McGRAW-HILL's

CONQUERING THE NEW GRE VERBAL AND WRITING

McGRAW-HILL's

CONQUERING THE NEW GRE VERBAL AND WRITING

Kathy A. Zahler, M.S.
Judy Unrein

1 2 3 4 5 6 7 8 9 10 11 12 QDB/QDB 1 9 8 7 6 5 4 3 2 1

ISBN   978-0-07-149598-1
MHID   0-07-149598-3

McGraw-Hill books are available at special quantity discounts to use as premiums and sales promotions, or for use in corporate training programs. To contact a representative, please e-mail us at bulksales@mcgraw-hill.com.

GRE is a registered trademark of Educational Testing Service, which was not involved in the production of, and does not endorse, this product.

POWERPREP II is a registered trademark of Educational Testing Service.

Cataloguing-in-Publication Data is on file with the Library of Congress.

CONTENTS

PART IV
GRE ANALYTICAL WRITING AND VERBAL REASONING
PRACTICE TESTS / 159

PART I
GETTING STARTED

CHAPTER 1

THE GRE ANALYTICAL WRITING AND VERBAL REASONING SECTIONS

CHAPTER GOALS

• Learn about the two Analytical Writing essay-writing tasks.

• Learn about the GRE Verbal Reasoning question types.

• Study examples of essay-writing prompts and Verbal question types.

The Graduate Record Examination (GRE) General Test does not test a specific content area. It tests your comprehension, math, and reasoning skills. Verbal skills—writing and reading and interpreting written material—take up the lion's share of the test. You will read given texts and be asked to respond to questions about them, you will analyze and complete sentences, you will apply your knowledge of English vocabulary in context, and you will write analytically. In other words, you will employ the sorts of critical thinking skills that graduate students use every day, no matter what discipline they undertake.

GRE FORMAT

The GRE revised General Test administered starting in August 2011 is available in two formats: a computer-based test and a paper-based test. The computer-based test is offered in the United States, Canada, and many other countries. The paper-based test is offered in areas of the world where computer-based testing is not available.

Whether computer-based or paper-based, the GRE includes these sections:

• **Analytical Writing:** This section includes two essay-writing tasks called "Analyze an Issue" and "Analyze an Argument."
• **Verbal Reasoning:** There are two scored Verbal Reasoning sections, each of which includes these question types: Sentence Equivalence,

Text Completion, and Reading Comprehension. Part III of this book deals with each kind of Verbal Reasoning question in detail.

- **Quantitative Reasoning:** There are two scored Quantitative Reasoning sections, each of which includes a mix of different kinds of math questions. Some questions are multiple-choice; others require you to calculate your own answer.

The computer-based test is partly *computer adaptive*. This term means that at certain points in the test, the computer decides what questions to give you based on your performance thus far. Specifically, if you perform well on the first Verbal Reasoning section, the computer will give you a second Verbal Reasoning section that is more difficult than the one you would have gotten if you did not perform well. The same procedure is followed for the two Quantitative Reasoning sections. Within each section, however, the test is not computer adaptive; a specific set of questions is presented in a specific order. Within a section you are free to skip questions or to move forward or backward through the question order as you wish.

> **FORMAT TIP**
>
> To answer a multiple-choice question on the computer-based GRE, first click the oval or square beside your answer choice. Then click either "Next" to go to the next question or "Back" to return to the previous question.

You will have 3 hours and 45 minutes to complete the entire test, including the Quantitative (math) section and any unscored sections. You will always begin with the two Analytical Writing tasks. You will complete each essay using the word processor that is part of the GRE software.

The charts that follow show the time breakdown for the sections of the test. Except for the Analytical Writing, which is always first, the sections may appear in any order. If there is an unscored Research section, it will always be last.

The following charts show the formats of the computer-based and paper-based GRE revised General Test.

Typical Computer-Based Revised General Test

Section	Number of Questions	Time
Analytical Writing	1 "Analyze an Issue" task 1 "Analyze an Argument" task	30 minutes per task
Section 1: Verbal Reasoning	Approximately 20 questions	30 minutes
Section 2: Verbal Reasoning	Approximately 20 questions	30 minutes
Section 3: Quantitative Reasoning	Approximately 20 questions	35 minutes
Section 4: Quantitative Reasoning	Approximately 20 questions	35 minutes

Typical Paper-Based Revised General Test

Section	Number of Questions	Time
Section 1: Analytical Writing	"Analyze an Issue" task	30 minutes
Section 2: Analytical Writing	"Analyze an Argument" task	30 minutes
Section 3: Verbal Reasoning	Approximately 25 questions	35 minutes
Section 4: Verbal Reasoning	Approximately 25 questions	35 minutes
Section 5: Quantitative Reasoning	Approximately 25 questions	40 minutes
Section 6: Quantitative Reasoning	Approximately 25 questions	40 minutes

An unidentified unscored section may be included at any point in the test. An identified un-scored research section may also be included at the end of the test.

GRE ANALYTICAL WRITING TASKS

The Analytical Writing measure consists of two tasks: Analyze an Issue (the Issue Task) and Analyze an Argument (the Argument Task). You must provide an essay to address each task. For each one, you will be given a single prompt and must respond directly to that prompt. Here are examples of each kind of prompt.

Issue Task

"It is often too easy to confuse power with greatness."

Discuss the extent to which you agree or disagree with the preceding claim. Use relevant reasons and examples to support your point of view.

Argument Task

A local school board put out this press release:

"Five years ago, we introduced the award-winning *Basic Math for Winners* as the math textbook to be used throughout our high school. Since that time, our four-year graduation rate has increased from 78 percent to 85 percent. It seems clear that this change in textbook has improved our academic success rate here at Markles Flats School District, and we look forward to purchasing *Basic Math for Winners* for our middle school students as well."

Critique the reasoning used in this argument by examining assumptions, assessing evidence, and/or suggesting ways to make the argument stronger or easier to evaluate.

Strategies to assist you with essay writing appear in Chapter 10, "GRE Analytical Writing."

GRE VERBAL REASONING QUESTION TYPES

The Verbal Reasoning sections of the GRE General Test include three main types of questions. There is no set number of each question type on the test, nor can the order of questions be predicted. Strategies to assist you with each of these question types appear in Chapters 7 through 9. The following are examples of each type.

Sentence Equivalence

Select *two* answer choices that (1) complete the sentence in a way that makes sense and (2) produce sentences that are similar in meaning.

Given her usual need for attention, we were _____ when Carole celebrated her birthday quietly and alone.

- A perturbed
- B optimistic
- C unconcerned
- D taken aback
- E enlightened
- F dumbfounded

The answers that create two coherent sentences with similar meanings are choices D and F.

Text Completion

Complete the text by picking the best entry for each blank from the corresponding column of choices.

The very first Russian *Matrioshka,* or nesting doll, was created in a workshop in Moscow in 1890. Russia was going through a period of artistic (i) _____. Artisans were searching for a new, (ii) _____ Russian craft.

Blank (i)	Blank (ii)
A doldrums	D distinctively
B revitalization	E politically
C prudence	F comprehensively

The answers that best complete the sentences are choices B and D.

READING COMPREHENSION

Read the passage and choose the best answer for each question.

Most people know that Francis Scott Key wrote "The Star-Spangled Banner." Many of those people know it was written during the Battle for Fort McHenry in the War of 1812. However, this is where popular knowledge typically ends.

One unusual fact about the American national anthem's history is that the tune to which it is set was not an original composition for the song. In fact, the music originated as a festive British folk song. Another is that while the song was composed and became popular in the first part of the nineteenth century, it was not treated as a song representing the United States for some time thereafter. At the first "modern" Olympics in 1896, it was played for American athletes, but it was not adopted as the country's official song until 1931.

Which of the following best states the author's main point?

(A) The national anthem evolved from a song that celebrated war.

(B) "The Star-Spangled Banner" was first sung at the Olympics.

(C) There are facts about our national anthem that we may not know.

(D) Our national anthem is really an old British folk song.

(E) Many popular songs have a long and interesting history.

The answer that best expresses the passage's main idea is choice C.

FORMAT TIP

You may skip questions, marking them in order to return to them later. A review screen allows you to see at a glance which questions you have not yet answered.

CHAPTER 2

SCORING ANALYTICAL WRITING AND VERBAL REASONING

CHAPTER GOALS

- Learn how the Analytical Writing essays are scored.

- Learn how the Verbal Reasoning sections are scored.

- Find out how to submit scores to schools.

Admissions departments or fellowship administrators may use your scores to compare your qualifications to those of other applicants. It is in your best interest to understand how the GRE is scored. There will be parts of your GRE that are not scored; a pretest is included to analyze questions for possible inclusion on upcoming tests, and a research section may also be included. You will not know whether the questions you are answering will count toward your score or not, so always assume that they will.

HOW YOUR ANALYTICAL WRITING ESSAYS ARE SCORED

Two trained readers employed by Educational Testing Service (ETS) will read each of your essays. They will use a six-point scale developed by ETS to grade your writing. The scoring is holistic, which means that you are graded on the overall quality of your writing rather than on a checklist of specific points. Chapter 10 contains specific information on the six-point scale used by the essay readers.

Beginning in 2012, your essay will be evaluated by a single human reader and an e-rater, which is a computer program designed by Educational Testing Service to monitor readers' scoring. If this computerized score matches the human score, the original score is used. If it disagrees significantly, a second trained reader will be called in to score the essay, and the final score will be the average of the two readers' scores.

Once both essays are scored, the average of those scores is used as the score for the Analytical Writing section. Based on statistics released by the Educational Testing Service, a score of 4.5 was approximately the median for students taking the GRE in the years 2002–2004.

It's important to note that Educational Testing Service uses software to search for plagiarism. They will apply this software to your essay. Only original work is acceptable.

HOW THE VERBAL REASONING SECTIONS ARE SCORED

Your score on the Verbal Reasoning sections of the test (and also on the Quantitative Reasoning sections) will depend on your specific performance on the questions given as well as the number of questions answered correctly in the allotted time. First, for each measure, a raw score is computed based on the number of questions answered correctly. Then, using statistical methods, each raw score is converted to a scaled score that takes account of small differences between test forms. For the computer-based test, the conversion process also takes account of the fact that the test is partially adaptive; that is, depending on how well you perform on the first Verbal and first Quantitative section, the computer may give you a second Verbal or Quantitative section that is more difficult. The purpose of statistically generating a scaled score is to make sure that scores achieved by test takers on one GRE test form are comparable to the same scores achieved on other GRE test forms. The Verbal and Quantitative scores are each reported on a 130–170 score scale, in 1-point increments. If you answer no questions at all in either section, a No Score (NS) is reported.

After you finish this book, it's worth trying some sample tests using the official POWERPREP II® software. This software scores your sample tests using the same complex scoring system that the official GRE exam uses. Using POWERPREP II, you can get a real sense of how you might score on the exam itself. You can download POWERPREP II from the GRE website: www.ets.org/gre.

HOW TO SUBMIT YOUR SCORES

At the time that you take the computer-based GRE, you may choose up to four institutions of higher learning or fellowship organizations to receive your score report. (If you take the paper-based test on paper, you may designate recipients when you register.) About two weeks after you complete the exam, your scores will be sent to you and to the institutions you selected. (This time period is closer to six weeks for paper-based tests and may be longer than that for any tests taken during the introductory test period between August and October 2011. If you need your scores before November 2011, you should take the *old* GRE test prior to August 2011.)

After you have received your scores, you may choose to send results to additional recipients. You may request this by phone by calling

1-888-GRE-SCORE (U.S., U.S. territories, and Canada) or 1-609-771-7290 (all others). You will need a credit card; there is a fee for each additional score report. You will also need your registration or confirmation number and the institution and department codes for the recipients you chose. The codes are available on the ETS website: www.ets.org/Media/Tests/GRE/pdf/gre_1011_tclist.pdf.

CHAPTER 3
GRE ACTION PLANS

CHAPTER GOALS

• Learn how to assess your test-taking needs.

• Make a schedule to train for the GRE General Test.

Reading this book cover to cover is probably not the best use of your time. You need an action plan that will help you to use the multifaceted information that's in here in a way that is personalized to your own test-taking needs.

ASSESS YOUR NEEDS

By this point in your life, you know how you study best for tests of this kind. You may be someone who benefits from study groups. You may work best alone. You may need help with Text Completions, but the other aspects of Verbal Reasoning may come easily to you. You may speak English as a second language and therefore require additional assistance with writing.

This book is designed to help you determine those areas of Verbal Reasoning in which you need additional practice. As you move through the Drills in Part III, be sure to check your answers against the Answers and Explanations. Look for patterns in your incorrect answers. Do you consistently miss certain kinds of Reading Comprehension questions? Review that part of Chapter 5. Do you have trouble finding synonyms to complete Sentence Equivalence questions? Check your knowledge of the vocabulary in Chapter 4.

Do not waste time on skills you have already mastered. Do make sure that you understand both the format used on the test and the test directions for each section. Spend your practice time on those skills that are difficult for you.

MAKE A TRAINING SCHEDULE

Studying for the GRE General Test will seem less daunting if you break it into manageable steps.

Step 1 is to register for the test and make your appointment with the Testing Center. The easiest way to do this is to go online to www.ets.org/gre. You will find a list of Testing Centers, a calendar of test dates, and registration forms.

Step 2 should take place about four weeks before your test date. Start working through the Drills in Part III of this book. Make note of the types of questions that seem most difficult for you. Continue this step each day for a week or two.

Step 3 should take place about three weeks before your test date. Go to the "Prepare for the Test" section of www.ets.org/gre and review the sample questions and the pool of writing topics. Any Analytical Writing you do on the test will be selected from the list of writing topics given on the website. It is worth taking the time to review those topics. If a topic does not make sense to you, talk it over with a friend until you understand it. Then take Sample Test 1 in Part IV of this book. Check your answers against the Answers and Explanations provided. Review the material in Parts II and III for any test items that caused you trouble.

Step 4 should take place about two weeks before your test date. Try one of the Practice Tests from POWERPREP II. Use the results to determine which sections in Parts II and III of this book you should review.

Step 5 should take place about one week before your test date. Take Sample Test 2 in Part IV of this book. Check your answers against the Answers and Explanations provided. Compare your results from Practice Test 2 to your results from Practice Test 1. Note your improvements and plan some quick review of any skills you still seem to lack.

On the final days before your test, concentrate on eating and sleeping well. Be sure that you have directions to the test site and can get there in ample time.

On test day, eat a good breakfast. Do breathing exercises or take a brisk walk before leaving for the Testing Center. Arrive with time to spare. When you finish the test, reward yourself with something you enjoy. Remember, it will take a couple of weeks to get the results, so put it out of your mind for now.

MY GRE TEST-PREP SCHEDULE

Test Center: _____

Date: _____ **Time:** _____

4 Weeks Before	Review Part III of this book:	
	Sentence Equivalence Drills	Results:
	Text Completion Drills	Results:
	Reading Comprehension Drills	Results:
	Analytical Writing: Issue	Results:
	Analytical Writing: Argument	Results:
3 Weeks Before	Review Sample Questions on www.ets.org/gre	Notes:
	Review Writing Topics on www.ets.org/gre	Notes:
	Take Practice Test 1 from this book	Results:
2 Weeks Before	Try a POWERPREP II test	Results:
	Review Parts II and III of this book	Notes:
1 Week Before	Take Practice Test 2 from this book	Results:
	Compare results to those from Practice Test 1	Notes:

My strengths: _____

Areas that need improvement: _____

_____

PART II
VERBAL FUNDAMENTALS

CHAPTER 4
VOCABULARY

CHAPTER GOALS

- Learn a few strategies for studying vocabulary.

- Identify and interpret Greek and Latin roots and affixes.

- Study a list of 300 vocabulary words.

- Use a specific strategy to decipher unfamiliar words.

A well-rounded vocabulary is absolutely essential to getting a good score on the GRE. About half of the questions in the Verbal Reasoning sections are solidly vocabulary based, and even the reading-based questions may prove a little easier if you know the definitions of the words you are reading.

People typically acquire vocabulary naturally through conversation and study. That may not be enough for your purposes here. To achieve the sophisticated, advanced vocabulary you need to succeed on the GRE, if you have not acquired it through natural means, will require concentrated study.

HOW TO STUDY VOCABULARY

Learning vocabulary is a lifelong pursuit, and no book can take the place of a lifetime of language acquisition. The exercises in this book are designed to help you identify those vocabulary words you need to study and then to give you a springboard into your personal practice.

Acquiring New Words

In addition to the words you learn from this book, you should always be on the lookout for more. If you're absorbing new words from several sources throughout the day, that constant focus will help you make connections between words, and you'll end up learning more, faster, and better. Here are some great sources of new words that you can access in your everyday life.

Word of the Day—There are many helpful e-mail services that will send you a vocabulary word every day, along with definitions, usage, and—depending on the service—memory devices and pronunciation. If you'd like to learn more than one word per day, there's nothing wrong with subscribing to several! Words of the day aren't just limited to e-mail; you can also get them via RSS feed and podcast if you're so inclined.

Reading—If you don't subscribe to any newspapers, start reading an article a day online. If you don't find challenging words in any of the big-name papers, choose from publications such as *The Economist, Science,* or *The Nation* and record unknown words using any of the methods described in the next section. Do the same with any reading that you do for work, school, or pleasure.

Listening—It's not always practical to ask someone what a word means when you hear it used in public, but if you write it down the way you think it's spelled, you'll probably be able to find it later, complete with its definition, in a print or online dictionary.

Recording New Words

Once you're in the habit of recording new vocabulary words, look up the definitions in a print dictionary or online source. One benefit of using online dictionaries is that you can easily and quickly access a variety of definitions. Typing "define: [word]" into Google also brings up a host of definitions in context.

Once you begin to pick up new words and find their definitions, there are a few ways to record them and expand that practice into your everyday life.

Flash Cards—Flash cards may remind you of kindergarten. Nevertheless, these old-fashioned cards still exist because they work—in part because they're incredibly flexible. You can make stacks of the words you already know and the ones you need to study. You can take the words you need to study with you on a plane or a bus or to work to review during some downtime. You can also shuffle the "already known" words back into the stack now and then to make sure that you don't forget them.

Your own personalized index cards are fine, but they're not the only option; there are lots of other ways to study using the flash card method. For example, there are many cheap or free flash card programs for Macs, PCs, and even handheld devices that let you input your words and definitions, test yourself, and exclude words that you already know; they are essentially electronic index cards. There are even a number of free online services that do the same thing. Just type "vocabulary flash cards" into your favorite search engine and see what pops up.

You can also buy premade flash cards with particular word sets. If you are short on time, these can be great, but there is definitely a benefit to making the cards yourself; just the act of creating the cards helps you study. This chapter will give you several ways to customize your flash cards based on associations you already have, so if you do buy a premade set, pick one that is easy to add information to, including some blank cards for words that you pick up along the way.

Once you pick a flash card method, what do you do? Obviously, you write the vocabulary word on one side and the definition on the other, but you can take this a step further. In addition to the definition, customize your cards by adding a memory device of some sort, so that every time you flip the card to check the definition you also get a reminder of how to remember it. You'll learn some helpful memory devices later in this chapter.

Vocabulary Notebook—Not everyone likes to study vocabulary in such a structured way. A notebook allows you the flexibility of writing lists of words, or writing and drawing, or making connections between different words by drawing lines and word webs. You can incorporate a strong visual element, so that when a word that you've studied shows up in your reading or on an exam, you can mentally flip to that page in your notebook and see your thoughts, your associations, and the definition. A notebook is also a very portable item, and it's easy to add new words to your notebook the moment you hear them.

Spreadsheet—In contrast, some people are *very* structured in their vocabulary study. If you learn best when everything lines up in neat rows, consider typing your word list into a spreadsheet program. You might use these columns: Word, Part of Speech, Definition, Memory Device, and Know?. (You can type Y or N in each Know? cell and then sort and filter to your heart's content.) A spreadsheet can be particularly helpful if you want to export your word list into a software-based flash card program, too.

Memory Devices

As you can see, many of the methods of keeping track of your vocabulary words encourage repetition. Repetition is good; in fact, it's essential for memorization. Nevertheless, reading the words and definitions over and over is only going to take you so far; it won't be long before you feel overwhelmed and start to forget the words you learned yesterday or last week. That can be true particularly when you're trying to learn large numbers of words. So you need something to take your studying to the next level.

Memory devices are tools that help you connect a word you are trying to learn with its definition—and then commit that connection to memory. There are many types of memory devices. Six appear here, but anything that helps you remember a word can be a memory device, whether it's an item on this list, a combination of several of these items, or something else entirely. Don't stick to just one kind of memory device when you study; the key is to choose devices that work for you and for the particular word you wish to recall.

Mnemonics—The word *mnemonics* is sometimes used to mean any memory device, but it can also mean a memory device that relates to how the word *sounds*. If a particular word sounds like another word you know, or a combination of words you know, you can make a mnemonic out of it.

For example, the word *ribald* means "marked by coarse or bawdy joking." If you can picture a clownish *bald* man telling *rib*-tickling jokes, you've created a mnemonic way of remembering the definition. The words *rib* and *bald* have absolutely nothing to do with *ribald,* but the mnemonic device can plant something in your mind that helps you retrieve the definition every time you see the word.

Rhymes—Anything that rhymes is going to stick in your head—that's why advertising agencies come up with so many rhyming slogans. You don't have to be a poet to create a rhyme; you can use something as simple as two words that rhyme and have similar meanings or a more extended couple of lines. For example, *laconic* means "using few words" and can describe a person, a written work (such as a speech or a story), or a style of writing. Here's a rhyme to help you remember *laconic*:

> The witness was so laconic,
> We gave him a talking tonic.

To create a rhyme, just think of a few words that rhyme with your word, pick one that you *could* relate to it, then fill in the rest with something relevant (such as a witness, whom you might prefer to be less laconic). No one else will see your rhymes, so don't worry if they're silly and the meter is awkward. Just make them memorable.

Illustrations—If you learn best tactilely or visually, or if you're simply learning words that bring pictures to your mind, go ahead and illustrate them. For example, you might draw someone "popping" in anger to illustrate the word *apoplexy,* which means "a fit of rage."

Associations—You can make associations in any of a wide range of ways. They're highly individual and highly effective. Just pick an association that works for you, and make sure you draw a connection to the definition. Here are some common types of associations:

Common phrases: If you're studying the noun *sanction,* you may remember that you often hear the phrase "imposed trade sanctions," and that can help you remember the definition, which is "a formal measure taken against a party to impose influence."

Movie quotes and song lyrics: When Wayne and Garth get suckered into an exploitative contract in the movie *Wayne's World*, Wayne says, "Let me *peruse* this contract carefully." *Peruse* means to examine in detail, and Wayne and Garth just sign the contract without reading it, which is what makes the moment funny. Because the line is part of a funny scene, you might very well recall the meaning of *peruse* the next time you read it. If you happen to be a theater buff, lines from a play can work the same way. To *inter* means "to bury"; hence, Shakespeare's line from *Julius Caesar*: "The evil that men do lives after them/The good is oft *interred* with their bones." Associating vocabulary with movies, plays, and songs is a good way to remember the meaning of unfamiliar words.

People or characters you know: To connect a word to a person, it's best to pick someone who personifies the word. For example, if you are studying the word *pejorative*, which means "contemptuous or disapproving," and you know someone who fits that description, great! If the person's name is Peggy, that's even better—now she is Pejorative Peggy, which is a memorable mnemonic.

Etymology—A word's *etymology* is its history or evolution. Some words do not derive from Greek or Latin roots but instead are references to famous people, authors, characters, events, or even cultural beliefs. Others could be phrases that became so common that after a few hundred years people just started saying them as a single word. When you look up a word in the dictionary, you will often find information about its roots or etymology or both. Knowing the etymology is like knowing a story about the word, and the more you know about the word, the better you'll be able to remember it. Some words with interesting etymologies are *Orwellian*, which is a reference to George Orwell's vision of a totalitarian future state; *gargantuan*, which means "huge" and is a reference to a fictional king with a huge capacity for food and drink; and *Lilliputian*, which means "miniature" and is a reference to the tiny people who tie up the hero of *Gulliver's Travels*. In the "words that got stuck together" category, there's *breakfast*, which is, literally, to *break* the *fast* you keep while you are sleeping, and *smog*, which is a portmanteau word combining *smoke* and *fog*.

Roots, Prefixes, and Suffixes—You will study these in detail later in this chapter, because once you know a few of these you will be able to figure out unfamiliar words when you have no access to a dictionary (during the GRE, for example). Figuring out definitions using word roots is not an exact science; because of the way in which the English language has evolved, sometimes it's possible to have prefixes that don't really change the meaning of a word (such as with *ravel* and *unravel*), words that appear to have one root but actually have a different one (such as *pedagogue,* which sounds as though it has to do with feet but which actually has to do with education), and words that appear identical but have two opposite meanings (such as *splice,* which can mean "to cut" or "to paste together"). However, these are the exceptions, not the rules, and for a test as vocabulary intensive as the GRE, it will definitely pay to know your roots.

With all these possible memory devices, you are sure to find at least one that works for each word you want to memorize. Don't be afraid to mix things up and use more than one means of memorizing vocabulary. Here are some examples:

> *Exculpate* means to free someone from blame or declare that someone is not guilty.

Here's a sentence that creates a mnemonic device:

> The *ex-culprit* was freed when new evidence cleared his name.

The sentence also creates an association with another word (*culprit*) because *culprit* and *exculpate* share a common root.

ROOTS AND AFFIXES

An extensive vocabulary clearly gives you an advantage in answering Text Completion and Sentence Equivalence questions. Studying this chart of common English-language roots and affixes will help you gain an understanding of the underpinnings of English vocabulary. Knowing roots and affixes can help you deduce the probable meanings of unfamiliar words.

Take, for example, the word *autonomy.* If you know that the prefix *auto-* means "self," you are halfway to understanding the meaning of the word, "self-sufficiency." Given the word *corporeal,* you could use your knowledge of the root *corp,* meaning "body," and guess at the meaning of the word, "bodily." Then there's the word *adductive.* The prefix *ad-* means "toward," the root *duct* means "to pull," and the suffix *-ive* means "having the quality of" and makes the word into an adjective. Put it all together, and you have "the quality of pulling toward," which is exactly what *adductive* means.

The chart that follows defines and gives examples of common Greek and Latin prefixes, suffixes, and roots. As you skim the chart, think about how the meaning of each word part contributes to the example words. Once you have a sense of how words are put together, you can apply what you know about word parts to interpret unfamiliar vocabulary.

Prefix	Meaning	Examples
a-, ac-, ad-, af-, ag-, al-, an-, ap-, as-, at-	to, toward, in addition to, according to	ahead, accompany, adhere, affix, aggravate, alarm, appall, assent, attempt
a-, an-	without	amoral, analgesic
ab-, abs-	away from	abdicate, absence
ante-	before	antebellum, anterior
anti-	against	antiwar, antipathy
auto-	self	automobile, autobiography
bi-	two	biannual, bicycle
circum-	around	circumnavigate, circumvent
co-, cog-, col-, com-, con-, cor-	with, together, mutually	coherent, cognizant, collapse, companion, concur, correspond
contra-	against, opposite	contradict, contravene
de-	to do the opposite of	decriminalize, degenerate
dis-	not, opposite of	disagree, disfavor
e-, ex-	out of, away from	egress, extension
em-, en-	to put into, to cause to be	endear, embody
epi-	upon, over	epidermis, epitaph
extra-	outside, beyond	extracurricular, extraordinary
il-, im-, in-, ir-	not	illicit, impossible, incorrect, irresponsible
inter-	between, among	intercom, international
intro-	into	introduce, introvert
mal-	bad	maladjusted, malformed
mis-	wrong	misnomer, misunderstood
mono-	one	monotone, monogamy
multi-	many	multifaceted, multimillions
non-	no, not	nonentity, nonsensical
ob-, oc-, of-, op-	toward, against	object, occlude, offend, opposite
over-	above, more than	overachieve, overcharge
para-	beside	paradigm, paragraph
per-	through, throughout	perambulate, permanent

Prefix	Meaning	Examples
peri-	around, about	peripatetic, periodic
post-	after	postdate, posthumous
pre-	before	prediction, preexist
pro-	for, supporting	procreate, promotion
re-	back, again	recall, recapture
retro-	backward	retrofit, retrospective
semi-	half	semicircle, semiconscious
sub-, suc-, suf-, sup-, sus-	below, under	subarctic, succumb, suffer, suppress, suspend
super-	over, above	superfluous, superscript
sur-	over, above	surpass, surrealism
sym-, syn-	together	sympathetic, synthesize
trans-	across	transatlantic, transmission
tri-	three	tricycle, trilogy
un-	not, opposite of	unlikely, unravel
uni-	one	uniform, unisex

Suffix	Function and Meaning	Examples
-able, -ible	adjective-forming; capable of, worthy of	laudable, flexible
-acy, -cy	noun-forming; state, quality	literacy, bankruptcy
-age	noun-forming; action	breakage, blockage
-al	adjective-forming; state, quality	communal, supplemental
-an, -ian	noun-forming; one who	artisan, librarian
-ance, -ence	noun-forming; action, state, quality	performance, adherence
-ancy, -ency	noun-forming; state, quality	buoyancy, fluency
-ant, -ent	noun-forming; one who or something that	deodorant, antecedent
-ant, -ent, -ient	adjective forming; indicating	compliant, dependent, lenient
-ar, -ary	adjective-forming; related to	solar, imaginary
-ate	verb-forming; cause to be	percolate, graduate
-ation	noun-forming; action	hibernation, strangulation

Suffix	Function and Meaning	Examples
-dom	noun-forming; place, condition	kingdom, freedom
-en	adjective-forming; made of	flaxen, wooden
-en	verb-forming; cause to be	cheapen, dampen
-er, -or	noun-forming; one who	painter, sailor
-fold	adverb-forming; divided or multiplied by	trifold, hundredfold
-ful	adjective-forming; full of	joyful, playful
-ful	noun-forming; amount	cupful, bucketful
-fy, -ify	verb-forming; cause to be	liquefy, justify
-ia	noun-forming; disease or condition of	inertia, anemia
-iatry	noun-forming; medical treatment	psychiatry, podiatry
-ic	adjective-forming; having the qualities of	futuristic, academic
-ician	noun-forming; one who	physician, mortician
-ics	noun-forming; science of	athletics, physics
-ion	noun-forming; action	completion, dilution
-ish	adjective-forming; having the quality of	foolish, boyish
-ism	noun-forming; doctrine	pacifism, jingoism
-ist	noun-forming; person who	jurist, polemicist
-ity, -ty	noun-forming; state, quality	reality, cruelty
-ive, -ative, -itive	adjective-forming; having the quality of	supportive, talkative, definitive
-ize	verb-forming; cause to be	demonize, dramatize
-less	without	careless, hopeless
-ly	adverb-forming; in the manner of	loudly, suddenly
-ment	noun-forming; action	argument, statement
-ness	noun-forming; state, quality	kindness, abruptness
-ous, -eous, -ose, -ious	adjective-forming; having the quality of	porous, gaseous, jocose, bilious
-ship	noun-forming; condition	scholarship, friendship

Suffix	Function and Meaning	Examples
-ure	noun-forming; action, condition	erasure, portraiture
-ward	adverb-forming; in the direction of	forward, windward
-wise	adverb-forming; in the manner of	otherwise, clockwise
-y	adjective-forming; having the quality of	chilly, crazy
-y	noun-forming; state, condition	jealousy, custody

Root	Meaning	Examples
ami, amo	to love	amiable, amorous
aud, audit, aur	to hear	audible, auditory, aural
bene, ben	good	benevolent, benign
bio	life	biography, biology
biblio	book	bibliography, bibliophile
brev	short	abbreviate, brevity
chron	time	chronology, synchronize
cogn, gnos	to know	cognitive, agnostic
corp	body	corpulent, corporation
cred	to believe	credible, incredulous
culp	fault, blame	culpable, exculpatory
dict	to say	indictment, dictation
doc, doct	to teach	docile, indoctrinate
duc, duct	to lead	conducive, induction
fac, fact	to make, to do	factory, efface
fid	belief	confide, fidelity
fluct, flux	to flow	fluctuation, influx
form	shape	format, cuneiform
fract, frag	to break	infraction, fragment
gen	to produce	generation, congenital
geo	earth	geographer, geology
grad, gress	to step, to move	graduate, ingress

Root	Meaning	Examples
graph	to write	photograph, graphics
ject	to throw	project, rejection
junct	to join	conjunction, adjunct
lect	to choose, to gather	select, collection
loc	place	locale, locomotion
log	to say	logical, analog
luc, lum, lust	light	lucid, luminous, illustrate
man	to make, to do	manager, manufacture
mem	to recall	remember, memorable
mit, miss	to send	remit, admission
mob, mov, mot	to move	mobile, remove, motion
nasc, nat	to be born	nascent, prenatal
nom, nym	name	nominal, homonym
nov	new	renovate, novice
oper	to work	operate, inoperable
path	feeling	empathy, sympathetic
ped, pod	foot	pedal, podiatrist
pel, puls	to push	repel, impulse
pend	to hang	pendant, impending
phil	love	philosophy, necrophilia
phon	sound	phonograph, telephone
pict	to paint	picture, depict
port	to carry	export, portage
psych	mind	psychology, psychic
quer, quest	to ask	query, request
rupt	to break	interrupt, rupture
scrib, scrip	to write	inscribe, script
sent, sens	to feel	sentient, sensation
sequ	to follow	sequence, consequential
soci	companion	society, associate
sol	alone	solo, solitude

Root	Meaning	Examples
solv, solu, solut	to loosen, to release	solve, soluble, solution
spec, spect	to look	special, inspection
spir	to breathe	spirit, respiration
stab, stat	to stand	stability, statue
tact	to touch	tactile, contact
tele	far	telescope, teleport
tend, tens	to stretch	extend, tensile
tain, tent	to hold	maintain, contents
term	end	terminal, exterminate
terr	earth	territory, subterranean
therm	heat	thermal, thermometer
tors, tort	to twist	torsion, contort
tract	to pull	contract, tractable
uni	one	universe, unicycle
vac	empty	vacuous, evacuate
ven, vent	to come	convene, venture
ver	true	verify, verisimilitude
verb	word	verbal, adverbial
vers, vert	to turn	reverse, convert
vid, vis	to see	video, invisible
vit, viv	to live	vital, convivial
voc, voke	to call	vocal, invoke
volv, volt, vol	to roll	volvox, revolt, convoluted

GRE VOCABULARY WORDS

There is no way to predict what words may turn up on the GRE General Test you take. That being said, there are certain words that seem to cause even good readers trouble, and those words provide a reasonable place to begin your vocabulary study. The chart that follows offers 300 vocabulary words with definitions and example sentences. Put the ones you don't know on flash cards, or study them directly from the chart.

The Sentence Equivalence portion of the GRE requires you to choose *two* words or phrases that complete a given sentence while producing similar or identical meanings. The "Definition" column of this chart offers some synonyms for difficult vocabulary words.

Word and Part of Speech	Definition	Example
abjure (v.)	to renounce or retract	He never did *abjure* his belief in the big bang theory.
abnegate (v.)	to renounce or give up	The king will *abnegate* power to his son, the prince.
accede (v.)	to agree to	Will the boss *accede* to her workers' demands?
accolade (n.)	praise; appreciation	My father won an *accolade* for bravery in wartime.
acrimonious (adj.)	bitter; spiteful	Their divorce was *acrimonious*; only the lawyers won.
adroitly (adv.)	skillfully; dexterously	Our waiter *adroitly* balanced several trays at once.
aegis (n.)	sponsorship; protection	He negotiated under the *aegis* of the prime minister.
altruistic (adj.)	charitable; generous	Giving away her favorite coat was an *altruistic* act.
ambience (n.)	setting or atmosphere	I like the *ambience* at that tiny corner café.
anodyne (adj.)	bland or soothing	The singsong music had an *anodyne* effect.
apostate (n.)	renegade; traitor	Having left the church, he was called an *apostate*.
asperity (n.)	roughness; harshness	She spoke with *asperity,* but her eyes were twinkling.
assiduous (adj.)	diligent; attentive	The carpenter was *assiduous* in lining up the corners.
auspices (n.)	sponsorship; support	The club functions under the *auspices* of the college.
avarice (n.)	greed	Midas lost his only daughter to his *avarice* for gold.
bacchanal (n.)	a drunken party	Chaperones kept the prom from being a *bacchanal*.
bastion (n.)	a fortress or defender	The D.A.'s office is our *bastion* against crime.

Word and Part of Speech	Definition	Example
beatific (adj.)	showing delight or bliss	Accepting her award, she gave a *beatific* smile.
behemoth (n.)	a huge, powerful thing	The elephant is the *behemoth* of the Indian forest.
bellicose (adj.)	quarrelsome; warlike	Separating the twins kept them from being *bellicose*.
bellwether (n.)	a leader or indicator	Housing foreclosures were a *bellwether* of recession.
benighted (adj.)	unenlightened	The *benighted* peasants thought the Earth stood still.
bevy (n.)	a group, esp. of girls	A *bevy* of young girls flowed through the mall.
bifurcate (adj.)	having two branches	The *bifurcate* stream flowed east and southeast.
blandishment (n.)	a flattering remark	She persuaded us both with *blandishment* and bribe.
boisterous (adj.)	energetic and noisy	The merry, *boisterous* crowd cheered on the team.
brigand (n.)	a thief or outlaw	That *brigand* was captured with the other pirates.
cajole (v.)	to coax or wheedle	You cannot *cajole* me to try that new restaurant.
canard (n.)	a false report	The suggestion that the senator is ill is just a *canard*.
celerity (n.)	speed	With great *celerity*, the rumor raced around town.
censure (n.)	disapproval; reprimand	The committee urged *censure* for his misconduct.
choleric (adj.)	bad-tempered	Her *choleric* nature kept the whole office on edge.
clemency (n.)	leniency; pardon	The judgment was harsh, but *clemency* was possible.
contumely (n.)	scornful treatment	Their *contumely* at his mistake was unbearable.
convivial (adj.)	fond of good times	A *convivial* person makes friends wherever she goes.
corporeal (adj.)	having physical form	Your *corporeal* assets may include houses or cars.
coterie (n.)	a close group of friends	My *coterie* loves to celebrate birthdays as a group.

Word and Part of Speech	Definition	Example
crux (n.)	a basic or deciding point	The *crux* of the matter seems to be affordability.
culpable (adj.)	blameworthy	Insurance companies were held *culpable* in his death.
cupidity (n.)	greed	Isn't *cupidity* one of the seven deadly sins?
deft (adj.)	skillful; dexterous	His *deft* fingers on the keyboard left us in awe.
deleterious (adj.)	harmful; injurious	Chemical additives may be *deleterious* to our health.
demagogue (n.)	a leader who appeals to passions and prejudices	A *demagogue* wins power by stirring up the people.
deprecate (v.)	to belittle	Do not *deprecate* my small attempts at humor.
derision (n.)	contempt; ridicule	Dr. Ding's peculiar theory was met with *derision*.
diaphanous (adj.)	sheer; gauzy	The dancers wore *diaphanous* skirts over leotards.
diffidence (n.)	a lack of self-confidence	People often mistook her *diffidence* for rudeness.
dissipate (v.)	to scatter; to disperse	The crowd will *dissipate* after the concert ends.
dolorous (adj.)	mournful; sad	That *dolorous* music brought tears to my eyes.
dotage (n.)	a feeble, aging mind	In his *dotage* he became more and more forgetful.
draconian (adj.)	excessively strict; harsh	Trespassing laws in this county are *draconian*.
dulcet (adj.)	sweet; melodious	We could hear the *dulcet* tones of her flute.
ebullience (n.)	enthusiasm; high spirits	The children's *ebullience* was delightful to see.
edict (n.)	a command or order	The king issued an *edict* demanding new taxes.
egregious (adj.)	flagrantly bad	Your rudeness toward the principal was *egregious*.
egress (n.)	an exit or way out	The nearest *egress* led through a door to the patio.
élan (n.)	enthusiasm; spirit	Her joyful *élan* is her most charming feature.

Word and Part of Speech	Definition	Example
elegiac (adj.)	expressing sorrow	His reading at the funeral was lovely and *elegiac.*
epicure (n.)	a person who enjoys good food and drink	I'm no *epicure,* but I do like visiting fine restaurants.
epitome (n.)	a typical example	Their ranch is the *epitome* of country living.
equivocal (adj.)	uncertain; undecided	The evidence was *equivocal* and led nowhere.
eschew (v.)	to shun; to avoid	Please *eschew* the passive voice in your writing.
euphonious (adj.)	pleasant-sounding	The chirping of the birds made a *euphonious* sound.
exalt (v.)	to praise; to glorify	That song was written to *exalt* the queen.
exhort (v.)	to urge or advise	Our professors *exhort* us to continue our studies.
expiate (v.)	to atone for	He worked in a soup kitchen to *expiate* his misdeeds.
expunge (v.)	to erase or delete	Can we *expunge* the record and start over again?
facile (adj.)	effortless; superficial	His answer was too *facile* for so complex a problem.
fallible (adj.)	likely to make mistakes	To be human is to be *fallible*; we all err at times.
fealty (n.)	allegiance; loyalty	Knights pledged an oath of *fealty* to their rulers.
fecund (adj.)	fertile; productive	Rabbits are quite *fecund* and produce many litters.
feign (v.)	to fake; to deceive	She may *feign* illness to avoid taking the test.
fervent (adj.)	showing great passion	It is my *fervent* hope that you will visit soon.
fetid (adj.)	foul-smelling	After three days in the heat, the garbage was *fetid.*
fidelity (n.)	loyalty or accuracy	This tape has great *fidelity* to the original recording.
filch (v.)	to steal	Did you *filch* my yogurt from the refrigerator shelf?
foist (v.)	to force upon slyly	He tried to *foist* his merchandise on innocent tourists.

Word and Part of Speech	Definition	Example
fortuitous (adj.)	happening by chance	Our meeting in the park was entirely fortuitous.
fulminate (v.)	to explode violently	His anger may fulminate if you continue to tease him.
fulsome (adj.)	offensively flattering	Her fulsome praise only made us mistrust her more.
gaffe (n.)	a foolish error	Joe's worst gaffe came when he called Lisa "Lucy."
galvanize (v.)	to rouse; to stimulate	His brave speeches always galvanize his listeners.
gargantuan (adj.)	enormous; gigantic	Three gargantuan derricks stood in the oil field.
genteel (adj.)	well-mannered; refined	At one time, a genteel woman always wore gloves.
germane (adj.)	relevant; to the point	Your opinion is not germane to this discussion.
gibe (v.)	to jeer or scoff at	They continued to gibe at the speaker until he quit.
glib (adj.)	smoothly superficial	Glib responses are inappropriate in serious times.
grandiloquence (n.)	pompous speech or writing	I prefer plain speaking to grandiloquence.
gratuitous (adj.)	free or without cause	Don't put up with that woman's gratuitous insults.
gustatory (adj.)	having to do with taste	Sweet things appeal to my gustatory senses.
hackneyed (adj.)	trite; overused	To use a hackneyed phrase, it'll knock your socks off!
halcyon (adj.)	peaceful and calm	The day was halcyon; not a cloud was in the sky.
hector (v.)	to bully; to boss around	Please don't hector your teammates unnecessarily.
heinous (adj.)	outrageously wicked	Supergluing his gloves together was a heinous act.
hermetic (adj.)	sealed tightly	If the flask is hermetic, no air will escape or enter.
heterodoxy (n.)	departure from tradition	Her heterodoxy upset the elders of the church.
hiatus (n.)	a break or interruption	My favorite TV show is on hiatus for the summer.

Word and Part of Speech	Definition	Example
hirsute (adj.)	hairy	Will the boy grow to be as *hirsute* as his father?
histrionic (adj.)	overly dramatic	With a *histrionic* gesture, she sent us on our way.
homily (n.)	a short sermon	In his *homily,* the pastor urged us to show respect.
humbug (n.)	a hoax or imposter	The Wizard of Oz was something of a *humbug.*
idyll (n.)	a short, pastoral poem	My professor read aloud an *idyll* by Tennyson.
ignominy (n.)	shame; disgrace	The captured criminals will now live in *ignominy.*
ilk (n.)	a type or class	People of that *ilk* rarely become managers.
impecunious (adj.)	poor; lacking money	Back then, most mine workers were *impecunious.*
imprecation (n.)	a curse or invocation of evil	The witch's *imprecation* doomed the princess.
incorrigible (adj.)	incapable of reform	The distressed counselor called the boy *incorrigible.*
ingratiate (v.)	to purposely gain favor	You might *ingratiate* yourself by praising her work.
inimitable (adj.)	matchless; unique	The *inimitable* style of his poetry cannot be copied.
iniquity (n.)	injustice or immorality	A "den of *iniquity*" is a place where evil is done.
insouciant (adj.)	carefree; casual	We could hear her *insouciant* whistling from indoors.
intrinsic (adj.)	inborn; essential	José seemed to have an *intrinsic* ear for music.
inveigh (v.)	to rail or complain about	Customers *inveigh* about the company's return policy.
irk (v.)	to irritate	If you *irk* him, he will toss you out of his office.
itinerant (adj.)	wandering	The *itinerant* laborer moved from town to town.
jejune (adj.)	dull; uninteresting	A *jejune* drama will not entertain this audience.
jeremiad (n.)	a long lament	The speech was a *jeremiad* about the evils of slavery.

Word and Part of Speech	Definition	Example
jibe (v.)	to change course	Our sailboat will *jibe* as it comes close to shore.
jocular (adj.)	joking; humorous	A *jocular* actor is best for the job of store Santa.
judicious (adj.)	careful and wise	His *judicious* plan appeased accused and accuser.
juggernaut (n.)	an unstoppable force	The storm was a *juggernaut* that crushed the town.
juxtapose (v.)	to place side by side	*Juxtapose* the photos to compare them more easily.
kinetic (adj.)	energetic; in motion	The *kinetic* sculpture turns slowly on its base.
kismet (n.)	fate; destiny	Running into each other at the mall was *kismet*.
kudos (n.)	praise	We offered *kudos* for her fine dance performance.
lachrymose (adj.)	weepy; mournful	Although her tale was *lachrymose*, it made us giggle.
lambaste (v.)	to reprimand or thrash	I will *lambaste* Carl for his unacceptable behavior.
lambent (adj.)	glowing softly	*Lambent* candles decorated each square window.
largesse (n.)	generosity or a gift	Our boss's *largesse* extended to extra vacation days.
laudable (adj.)	worthy of praise	Her focus on protecting our wetlands was *laudable*.
libation (n.)	an alcoholic drink	He poured a *libation* and toasted the New Year.
licentious (adj.)	immoral; debauched	*Licentious* material is banned from school computers.
limpid (adj.)	clear and bright	You could see to the bottom of the *limpid* stream.
lissome (adj.)	supple; agile	The dancers' *lissome* movements were soothing.
litany (n.)	a prolonged, dull recital	His *litany* of complaints did nothing to persuade us.
lithe (adj.)	supple; agile	With a *lithe* leap, the gymnast landed on the beam.
lugubrious (adj.)	excessively mournful	We nearly laughed at the dean's *lugubrious* tone.

Word and Part of Speech	Definition	Example
luminary (*n.*)	a celebrity or intellectual	We were joined by a *luminary* from the art world.
macerate (*v.*)	to break down or soak	The digestive system serves to *macerate* food.
mainstay (*n.*)	a chief support	Reading instruction is the *mainstay* of education.
martinet (*n.*)	a strict disciplinarian	My middle school principal was a stern *martinet*.
maudlin (*adj.*)	overly sentimental	Our great aunt sends us *maudlin* greeting cards.
meander (*v.*)	to twist or wander	Three slow streams *meander* through the property.
mellifluous (*adj.*)	sweet-sounding	The meadowlark has a pleasant, *mellifluous* song.
mendacity (*n.*)	dishonesty; falsehood	The man's *mendacity* will lead others to mistrust him.
mendicant (*n.*)	a beggar	A *mendicant* tugged at my coat and asked for help.
mercurial (*adj.*)	changeable	Her *mercurial* moods confused her roommates.
miasma (*n.*)	a poisonous vapor	A dank *miasma* rose from the flooded swamp.
mien (*n.*)	manner or appearance	At an interview, your *mien* should be professional.
misanthrope (*n.*)	a hater of humankind	No *misanthrope* should ever run for public office.
miscreant (*n.*)	a villain or criminal	Will the *miscreant* receive appropriate punishment?
modulate (*v.*)	to alter; to tone down	Please *modulate* your voice in the library.
moribund (*adj.*)	approaching death	Onondaga may be considered a *moribund* language.
munificent (*adj.*)	extremely generous	The *munificent* gift will build a new hospital wing.
mutable (*adj.*)	capable of change	Our opinions on the subject seem to be *mutable*.
nadir (*n.*)	the lowest point	The *nadir* of my career came when he fired me.
nebulous (*adj.*)	cloudy or vague	His explanation was *nebulous* and left us baffled.

Word and Part of Speech	Definition	Example
nefarious (adj.)	extremely wicked	The convict's *nefarious* crimes led to a life sentence.
nether (adj.)	located below or under	Colonial women wore layers of *nether* garments.
nexus (n.)	a link or connection	Drugs may be a *nexus* between terrorism and crime.
niggardly (adj.)	stingy; miserly	The broker left a *niggardly* tip of only fifty cents.
nihilism (n.)	the rejection of beliefs	Jude's *nihilism* contrasts with his priestly garments.
noisome (adj.)	harmful or foul-smelling	A *noisome* stench arose where we were digging.
nonplus (v.)	to bewilder; to perplex	Their carefree attitude might *nonplus* their elders.
nostrum (n.)	a remedy	The poet found love to be a *nostrum* for melancholy.
noxious (adj.)	harmful; toxic	Keep *noxious* chemicals out of the water supply.
nuance (n.)	a slight difference	Notice the *nuance* in color between the two scarves.
nugatory (adj.)	of little importance	His opinion was *nugatory* to the group's decision.
obeisance (n.)	a gesture of respect	The knight made humble *obeisance* before the duke.
obloquy (n.)	verbal abuse	Their *obloquy* seemed cruel and almost slanderous.
odious (adj.)	disgusting; offensive	His behavior is *odious,* and his speech is rude.
offal (n.)	garbage or entrails	Dress the deer and throw the *offal* into the woods.
onus (n.)	a burden or duty	Her grandfather's care is an *onus* she gladly bears.
ossify (v.)	to turn hard and bony	The dried gourds seemed to *ossify* in the hot sun.
ostracize (v.)	to banish or exclude	Do not *ostracize* him because he disagrees with you.
ouster (n.)	a forcible dispossession	After her *ouster* from the club, she considered suing.
overweening (adj.)	excessive or arrogant	His *overweening* ambition nearly took over his life.

Word and Part of Speech	Definition	Example
panache (*n.*)	elegance; style	Aunt Ida wore her purple feather boa with *panache*.
parity (*n.*)	equality	Have women achieved *parity* in intramural sports?
patois (*n.*)	a dialect	Many folks along the river speak a Creole *patois*.
peccadillo (*n.*)	a minor sin or offense	It was easy to forgive him for that mild *peccadillo*.
pedant (*n.*)	a small-minded teacher	I prefer a know-it-all to a rules-obsessed *pedant*.
penumbra (*n.*)	a partial shadow	We saw the moon's *penumbra* during the eclipse.
peregrination (*n.*)	a pilgrimage or journey	His *peregrination* took him many hundreds of miles.
perfidy (*n.*)	a betrayal or treachery	Benedict Arnold is now famous mostly for his *perfidy*.
phalanx (*n.*)	a close formation of troops; a crowd	The *phalanx* of horsemen closed in on the fortress.
picayune (*adj.*)	trivial or petty	Don't trouble me with those *picayune* details.
piquant (*adj.*)	spicy or stimulating	The sauce was smooth, with a *piquant* aftertaste.
plait (*n.*)	a braid	Sarah Jane wrapped her long *plait* around her head.
platitude (*n.*)	a cliché; a dull remark	No *platitude* is likely to engage the audience.
plebeian (*adj.*)	vulgar or common	She thought bowling was too *plebeian* a sport.
prosaic (*adj.*)	matter-of-fact; dull	He described his vacation in flat, *prosaic* terms.
provenance (*n.*)	origin; source	What is the *provenance* of this oil painting?
puissance (*n.*)	power; strength	The *puissance* of the unions led to that new law.
pulchritude (*n.*)	physical beauty	Are models supposed to be the height of *pulchritude*?
putative (*adj.*)	alleged; presumed to be	The *putative* author was later shown to be illiterate.
quaff (*v.*)	to drink deeply	We merrily *quaff* the punch at the office party.

Word and Part of Speech	Definition	Example
quagmire (*n.*)	a swamp or a sticky predicament	The *quagmire* of Vietnam sank several careers.
qualms (*n.*)	uneasiness	She had some *qualms* about hiring the whistle-blower.
quandary (*n.*)	a state of uncertainty	He was in a *quandary* about which job to take.
quay (*n.*)	a wharf; a dock	Sailors docked the ships at the *quay* for unloading.
quell (*v.*)	to suppress or alleviate	Crackers may *quell* our hunger for a while.
queue (*n.*)	a line waiting for service	The *queue* at the ticket booth was long and restless.
quiescence (*n.*)	dormancy; inactivity	The deer's *quiescence* ends with cooler weather.
quixotic (*adj.*)	idealistic; unrealistic	He has a *quixotic* belief in the goodness of humanity.
quotidian (*adj.*)	everyday	My *quotidian* routine has become deadly dull.
raffish (*adj.*)	dapper; dashing	He looked confident in his *raffish* scarf and cap.
rapacious (*adj.*)	predatory; greedy	The young lioness has quite a *rapacious* appetite.
raucous (*adj.*)	unpleasantly loud	Their *raucous* laughter kept the rest of us awake.
regale (*v.*)	to entertain or provide	Our host will *regale* us with food and conversation.
repast (*n.*)	a meal; a feast	A long walk will help us to digest that grand *repast*.
replete (*adj.*)	filled up; stuffed	Everyone was *replete* following the wedding feast.
respite (*n.*)	a break or relief	The long weekend was a welcome *respite* for all.
retinue (*n.*)	attendants; entourage	Rapper D never travels without a *retinue* of friends.
ribald (*adj.*)	bawdy; lewd	The comedian's jokes were *ribald* and shocking.
rife (*adj.*)	widespread; prevalent	Disease was *rife* in Europe during the Middle Ages.
rift (*n.*)	a crack or division	After the earthquake, a *rift* appeared in the field.

Word and Part of Speech	Definition	Example
riposte *(n.)*	a comeback or retort	Her clever *riposte* stopped his argument in its tracks.
rostrum *(n.)*	a platform or dais	The speaker stood behind a *rostrum* on the stage.
rue *(v.)*	to regret; to be sorry	You will *rue* the day that you angered my friend.
ruminate *(v.)*	to reflect deeply on	In class, we will *ruminate* on the theme of madness.
sagacious *(adj.)*	wise; perceptive	One hopes that one's professors will be *sagacious*.
salutary *(adj.)*	beneficial	Drinking water seems to be *salutary* to everyone.
sanguine *(adj.)*	optimistic; upbeat	He seemed oddly *sanguine* about the recession.
sardonic *(adj.)*	mocking; cynical	In a *sardonic* tone, she suggested we look elsewhere.
saturnine *(adj.)*	sluggish or gloomy	Joe was *saturnine,* but his wife was always cheerful.
schism *(n.)*	a split into factions	When did the *schism* in the Catholic Church occur?
sinecure *(n.)*	a job with few duties	His *sinecure* with the governor's office was a gift.
slake *(v.)*	to quench or satisfy	The hikers can *slake* their thirst at the ranger station.
sobriquet *(n.)*	a nickname	The *sobriquet* "Lumpy" does not describe her figure.
sophomoric *(adj.)*	immature	They regretted playing such a *sophomoric* prank.
sordid *(adj.)*	disgusting; nasty	I quickly returned the *sordid* magazine to the shelf.
spate *(n.)*	a sudden rush or flood	After a *spate* of e-mails, I heard nothing for weeks.
spurious *(adj.)*	false; illegitimate	Your argument is *spurious*; it lacks sense and logic.
stalwart *(adj.)*	hardy and loyal	Big Ben is a *stalwart,* obedient hunting dog.
steadfast *(adj.)*	firm and dependable	A *steadfast* employee is likely to be rewarded.
stoic *(adj.)*	impassive; inexpressive	The young boy was *stoic* as he received his flu shot.

Word and Part of Speech	Definition	Example
stymie *(v.)*	to obstruct; to hinder	One move helped the chess master *stymie* his rival.
succinct *(adj.)*	concise; to the point	Writing that is *succinct* is easier to understand.
supplicant *(n.)*	a beggar or petitioner	A *supplicant* stood palm upward beside the cathedral.
surmise *(v.)*	to guess or conclude	You might *surmise* that he is not a native speaker.
sycophant *(n.)*	a self-serving flatterer	The king laughed at the *sycophant* behind his back.
tactile *(adj.)*	having to do with touch	Reading Braille is *tactile* rather than visual.
taint *(v.)*	to infect or corrupt	Don't let prejudice *taint* your opinions and beliefs.
tautology *(n.)*	a needless repetition	It's a *tautology* to say "This may be true or untrue."
tawdry *(adj.)*	cheap and gaudy	Her *tawdry* outfit was better suited to a saloon.
temerity *(n.)*	foolish bravery	It took *temerity* to question his captain's orders.
terse *(adj.)*	abrupt or curt	He gave a *terse* reply to our lengthy question.
timorous *(adj.)*	fearful; timid	A mouse is *timorous* by nature, but a fox is sly.
toady *(n.)*	a self-serving flatterer	The *toady* was always ready with an oily compliment.
tome *(n.)*	a volume or large book	She lugged the weighty *tome* from the library.
torrid *(adj.)*	hot or passionate	They carried on a *torrid* correspondence for years.
tout *(v.)*	to recommend highly	I always *tout* her books to all of my friends.
traverse *(v.)*	to cross over	Are you allowed to *traverse* the bridge on foot?
travesty *(n.)*	a mockery	The trial was a *travesty*; the judge was half asleep.
trenchant *(adj.)*	keen or forceful	Oscar Wilde was known for his *trenchant* wit.
truculent *(adj.)*	ferociously defiant	His *truculent* speech won him new enemies.

Word and Part of Speech	Definition	Example
turbid (adj.)	cloudy; murky	The turbid water may hide many sharp rocks.
turpitude (n.)	vileness; depravity	Crimes of moral turpitude may lead to deportation.
ubiquitous (adj.)	present everywhere	Cell phones seem to be ubiquitous in high schools.
umbrage (n.)	resentment; offense	She took umbrage when I laughed at her dog.
unctuous (adj.)	oily in manner	His unctuous smile was obviously insincere.
undulate (v.)	to move in waves	The rattlesnake seemed to undulate over the sand.
unkempt (adj.)	disheveled; untidy	Please comb your unkempt hair before going out.
unsung (adj.)	not honored or valued	The soldier's bravery was unsung; he won no medal.
urbane (adj.)	refined; suave	Clyde seemed rather urbane after his tour abroad.
usurp (v.)	to seize; to take over	They cannot usurp power without support from us.
usury (n.)	charging of exorbitant interest	Some credit card companies seem to practice usury.
vacuous (adj.)	lacking intelligence	Her vacuous stare made her appear bored and silly.
vagary (n.)	an odd, unexpected act	A vagary in the weather dumped six inches of snow.
vainglorious (adj.)	boastful; self-important	She has no cause to act in such a vainglorious way.
valor (n.)	courage; heroism	Valor on the field of battle was crucial for a knight.
vanquish (v.)	to defeat; to overcome	Our debating team will vanquish all rival teams.
venal (adj.)	easily corrupted	A venal player might throw a game for money.
venerable (adj.)	respected or impressive	The venerable chief had ruled for nearly fifty years.
vicissitude (n.)	changeability	A vicissitude in fortune enabled him to go to college.

Word and Part of Speech	Definition	Example
vilify (v.)	to defame or belittle	The columnist tried to *vilify* the author in print.
virago (n.)	a quarrelsome woman	Katherina is a *virago* in *The Taming of the Shrew.*
virulent (adj.)	venomous; deadly	Anthrax is a disease caused by a *virulent* bacterium.
vitiate (v.)	to spoil or corrupt	Sudden wealth can *vitiate* a well-meaning person.
vitriol (n.)	cruel, bitter speech	I will not listen to such *vitriol* about my friend.
vituperate (v.)	to condemn or berate	No good coach should *vituperate* a losing team.
voluble (adj.)	talkative	Her *voluble* oration kept us from adding one word.
waft (v.)	to float or blow gently	Dead leaves *waft* on the cool autumn breeze.
wanton (adj.)	immoral or unjustified	*Wanton* cruelty to animals is always appalling.
waspish (adj.)	bad-tempered	Dinah's *waspish* personality irritated her sisters.
wastrel (n.)	a spendthrift	The young *wastrel* soon squandered his inheritance.
whet (v.)	to sharpen or arouse	Delicious kitchen odors may *whet* your appetite.
wily (adj.)	sly; cunning	My *wily* puppy found a way to open the pantry door.
winnow (v.)	to separate out	Wash the berries and *winnow* out any unripe ones.
wizened (adj.)	wrinkled; shriveled	Her *wizened* face seemed both wise and kindly.
wraith (n.)	a ghost; an apparition	The fog hung like a *wraith* over the churchyard.
xenophobia (n.)	the fear of foreigners	Severe *xenophobia* kept him from enjoying travel.
yammer (v.)	to talk continually	Must you *yammer* on about your troubles?
yaw (v.)	to swing back and forth	The plane might *yaw* as it flies through the storm.
yurt (n.)	a circular tent	My cousins lived in a *yurt* for the summer.

Word and Part of Speech	Definition	Example
zealous *(adj.)*	enthusiastic; fervent	Paul is a *zealous* fan of the Cleveland Browns.
zenith *(n.)*	the highest point	At the *zenith* of their climb, they saw the sea below.
zephyr *(n.)*	a gentle, warm breeze	A constant *zephyr* warms their island home.
ziggurat *(n.)*	a terraced pyramid	The Mayans built a *ziggurat* overlooking the ocean.

Try It Yourself

For each of the following, take a guess at the definition of the boldfaced words from context, your prior knowledge, and your understanding of roots, prefixes, and suffixes. Then jot down a quick association if you have heard the word before. Finally, look up each word in a dictionary to see how close your guess was, and think up a memory device to help you remember the definition. If the charts in items 1–4 help you, copy them to use for items 5–50.

1. Orly's directions to the soccer fields were completely **ambiguous**; I could interpret them in so many different ways that they **impeded** my attempts to get there rather than helping me.

    ambiguous

    my guess: _____

    my association: _____

    part of speech: _____ dictionary definition: _____

    memory device: _____

    impede

    my guess: _____

    my association: _____

    part of speech: _____ dictionary definition: _____

    memory device: _____

2. Orly admits that he is **maladroit** at giving directions under the best circumstances; however, that is **exacerbated** by the fact that he is new to town and barely knows his own way around.

maladroit

my guess: _____

my association: _____

part of speech: _____ dictionary definition: _____

memory device: _____

exacerbate

my guess: _____

my association: _____

part of speech: _____ dictionary definition: _____

memory device: _____

3. An atmosphere of **antipathy** seemed to **permeate** the campus on the weekend we played against the Springfield State Panthers, our biggest rivals.

antipathy

my guess: _____

my association: _____

part of speech: _____ dictionary definition: _____

memory device: _____

permeate

my guess: _____

my association: _____

part of speech: _____ dictionary definition: _____

memory device: _____

4. Whenever we play the Panthers, even a tradition as **innocuous** as a pep rally can cause a **conflagration** of hostility among the students.

innocuous

my guess: _____

my association: _____

part of speech: _____ dictionary definition: _____

memory device: _____

conflagration

my guess: _____

my association: _____

part of speech: _____ dictionary definition: _____

memory device: _____

5. The prosecutor's attempts to **nonplus** the defendant were ultimately **abortive**; either he had been coached extremely well to be on the witness stand or he was simply confident in his innocence.

6. Finally the prosecutor became so desperate that he resorted to **blatant** harassment, and the attorney for the defense loudly lodged an **ardent** objection.

7. The credit card company has **draconian** policies by most standards; even one **delinquent** payment can double a cardholder's interest rate and result in huge fees.

8. Now the company has been ordered by a court to **remunerate** some cardholders who paid late once but were by no means **lackadaisical** customers.

9. Diana's lack of confidence in her supervisory skills causes her to reply in an **astringent** way to those who seem to **gainsay** her directives.

10. Her **moratorium** on laughter during staff meetings, though, was what caused her staff to start calling her **pejorative** names, such as Dictator Diana, behind her back.

11. The normally **lethargic** city council is finally taking action in response to the **waxing** public anger about the number of accidents at Third and Oak streets.

12. The public has made it clear that the **ramifications** for inaction on this issue will be **dire**.

13. Raul's attempts to **delve** into the case were **futile**, as it was difficult to get a straight answer from the only eyewitness.

14. The eyewitness only gave **enigmatic** replies, flatly refusing to be concerned that his **intractability** was preventing the case from ever coming to court.

15. After spending the day in crowded malls, Gayle found the **sanctuary** of a shaded park a welcome **respite**.

16. The subtle fragrance of flowers and grass formed a **gratifying** contrast to the overpowering **redolence** of the perfume counter at which she worked.

17. After much debate, the senator was forced to admit that his plan was simply **chimerical**, **devoid** of any real basis in solid public policy.

18. Once the bill had been withdrawn, time pressures made it necessary to **draft** a replacement with a greater sense of **exigency** than before.

19. The coming of spring seems to **infuse** everyone with a sense of **joviality**, particularly after a long or harsh winter.

20. **Vernal** delights such as blossoming plants and longer days with more sunshine can make even the most dedicated **stoic** more cheerful.

21. The **climactic** moment of the play isn't until the **penultimate** scene, so the audience gets only one short scene of wrap-up after the main action.

22. Under close **scrutiny**, though, the playwright's intentions become clear: she doesn't tie up loose ends very well because she wants the audience to leave with a sense of **disquiet**.

23. The menu was clearly drawn from a **mélange** of **disparate** sources, as Indian, Mediterranean, and American Southwest dishes were all represented.

24. It would have been easy for the selections to seem like a scattered assortment, but under the chef's **savvy** direction, the dishes chosen appeared perfectly **attuned** to each other.

25. The soft music programmed on the concert would have had a **somnolent** effect were it not for a single **aleatory** element: occasionally the piano seemed out of tune.

26. To **demystify** the cause, the composer indicated in the program notes that a soft ball should be placed in the strings of the piano to produce **discordant** sounds.

27. Sara's brief visit to a smelly pig farm, though **cursory**, convinced her that she could never live in such a **noisome** environment.

28. Having grown up around horses, she found that she far preferred **equine** smells to the **porcine** ones at the pig farm.

29. The **putative** cause of Marco's dismissal was the prank he had played on his boss the week before, for which he **naïvely** believed he would not be punished.

30. Most of his coworkers, however, were unaware that he had been found guilty of a far more **grievous** infraction: he had **filched** over a thousand dollars out of various cash registers.

31. Carmen's frustration with her husband's **frugality** finally came to a head when he refused to spend five more dollars for a nonstop flight, and she called him a **parsimonious** miser.

32. His response was that they wouldn't have to worry so much about money if Carmen were not such an **edacious spendthrift**.

33. Ari was known as a **mugwump** to his friends who liked to discuss politics; however, this senatorial race is so heated that even he will **opine** that the incumbent must go.

34. He tells anyone who will listen that the current senator is a **jingoist**, and the time has come for politicians who have the sense to be **pacifists** and diplomats.

35. Shahira enjoys spending summers on the lake, where she may **placidly** enjoy the scenery and silence, away from the constant **clamor** of the city.

36. Her children, however, have more **urbane** tastes; they think that life away from the comforts of the city is a little too **rustic**.

37. Josh seems distant, but those close to him know that his **aloofness** is just a **façade**.

38. Clearly Josh's insecurities **manifest** themselves in ways that make him seem cold and **dispassionate**.

39. The normally **brusque** critic for the local paper is **profuse** with admiration for the sculptor's new exhibit.

40. Frankly though, I don't think it deserves that much **adulation**; while technically stunning, it is not at all as artistically **nuanced** as his previous work.

41. Clouds on the horizon may very well **portend** rain, but rarely are they **harbingers** of tornadoes.

42. Should those clouds be coupled with a tornado siren, however, it is **foolhardy** not to assume that you are in **imminent** danger.

43. Rarely have I met such an **egocentric** individual as Howard; any topic of conversation will **induce** him to start a story about one of his fabulous adventures.

44. As our friends will **attest**, he once spent half an hour telling us how he was considered the **epitome** of a model student and athlete in high school.

45. The collection of volumes in the library is so **eclectic** that I suspect one could find books on even the most **arcane** of topics.

46. However, gaining access to the collection is hardly a **nominal** task; all but the most respected scholars typically have to **grovel** at the librarian's feet to gain admission.

47. The small town on the edge of the woods attracts many tourists who brave losing themselves on **Byzantine** trails to enjoy the **sylvan** landscapes.

48. For visitors who love **exotic** food, though, the town's two restaurants, a diner and a steak house, seem rather **pedestrian**.

49. Harriet's long-standing **melancholia** has isolated her, making her something of a social **pariah** among those who prefer cheerier companionship.

50. Though she has tried lately to be more cheerful, even the most **altruistic** of her acquaintances considers her a hopeless **curmudgeon**.

▨ VOCABULARY DRILL

For each exercise, match one word on the left with the word on the right that is closest in meaning. Keep an eye on the part of speech of each word; match verbs to verbs, nouns to nouns, and adjectives to adjectives. Answers appear after the drill.

1. ascetic   inculpate

   preclude   sardonic

   incriminate   condone

   sanction   abstemious

   acerbic   obviate

2. attenuate   verify

   calumny   assuage

   ascertain   dilemma

   quandary   eschew

   spurn   denigration

3. clemency   gratuitous

   nugatory   trifling

   fulsome   noxious

   injurious   leniency

   unwarranted   immoderate

4. wraith   novice

   asperity   culpable

   jocose   specter

   neophyte   facetious

   blameworthy   curtness

5. inveigh   acrimonious

    abnegate   hermetic

    dissolute   rail

    airtight   debauched

    rancorous   renounce

6. lugubrious   bypass

    bellicose   somber

    censure   laudable

    circumvent   combative

    commendable   rebuke

7. egress   garrulous

    voluble   lithe

    archetype   mutable

    lissome   outlet

    fluctuating   paradigm

8. schism   inane

    trenchant   alacrity

    vacuous   caustic

    miscreant   rupture

    celerity   malefactor

9. succumb   malign

    vilify   divert

    cantankerous   capitulate

    hackneyed   trite

    regale   choleric

10. adhere   idealistic

    obstreperous   truculent

    nefarious   eradicate

    annihilate   reprehensible

    quixotic   affix

Answers and Explanations

1. Both *ascetic* and *abstemious* mean "strict" or "frugal." *Preclude* and *obviate* mean "prevent." *Incriminate* and *inculpate* mean "lay blame on." *Sanction* and *condone* mean "approve." *Acerbic* and *sardonic* mean "biting" or "sharp."

2. Both *attenuate* and *assuage* mean "satisfy." *Calumny* and *denigration* mean "slander." *Ascertain* and *verify* mean "make sure" or "prove." *Quandary* and *dilemma* mean "sticky situation." *Spurn* and *eschew* mean "reject."

3. Both *clemency* and *leniency* mean "mercy." *Nugatory* and *trifling* mean "unimportant." *Fulsome* and *immoderate* mean "excessive." *Injurious* and *noxious* mean "harmful." *Unwarranted* and *gratuitous* mean "unnecessary."

4. Both *wraith* and *specter* mean "ghost." *Asperity* and *curtness* mean "harshness." *Jocose* and *facetious* mean "joking." *Neophyte* and *novice* mean "beginner." *Blameworthy* and *culpable* mean "at fault."

5. Both *inveigh* and *rail* mean "complain bitterly." *Abnegate* and *renounce* mean "give up." *Dissolute* and *debauched* mean "having loose moral standards." *Airtight* and *hermetic* mean "sealed." *Rancorous* and *acrimonious* mean "full of resentment."

6. Both *lugubrious* and *somber* mean "gloomy." *Bellicose* and *combative* mean "eager to fight." *Censure* and *rebuke* mean "scold" or "reprimand." *Circumvent* and *bypass* mean "go around." *Commendable* and *laudable* mean "worthy of praise."

7. Both *egress* and *outlet* mean "a way out." *Voluble* and *garrulous* mean "talkative." *Archetype* and *paradigm* mean "model." *Lissome* and *lithe* mean "agile" or "flexible." *Fluctuating* and *mutable* mean "changing."

8. Both *schism* and *rupture* mean "split." *Trenchant* and *caustic* mean "biting." *Vacuous* and *inane* mean "silly." *Miscreant* and *malefactor* mean "evildoer." *Celerity* and *alacrity* mean "speed."

9. Both *succumb* and *capitulate* mean "give in." *Vilify* and *malign* mean "badmouth." *Cantankerous* and *choleric* mean "irritable." *Hackneyed* and *trite* mean "clichéd." *Regale* and *divert* mean "entertain."

10. Both *adhere* and *affix* mean "stick." *Obstreperous* and *truculent* mean "disobedient." *Nefarious* and *reprehensible* mean "wicked." *Annihilate* and *eradicate* mean "get rid of." *Quixotic* and *idealistic* mean "unrealistically romantic."

Sanction
Condone

CHAPTER 5

READING COMPREHENSION

CHAPTER GOALS

- Learn specific strategies for improving Reading Comprehension.

- Review the reading skills tested in Reading Comprehension questions.

Reading Comprehension on the GRE consists of 12 to 15 passages, most of them a single paragraph in length, followed by questions in one of three formats. The passages are nonfiction and may be on topics from the humanities, from social sciences, or from natural sciences. The expectation is that you will not be familiar with the content of a given passage or that, if you are familiar with it, you will not be an expert.

For this reason, it is not possible to *study* for the Reading Comprehension section of the GRE. That being said, however, there are some things you may do to *prepare* for it.

PREPARING FOR READING COMPREHENSION

By this stage in your educational career, you should have a pretty good sense of your test-taking skills. If you have achieved solid scores on reading comprehension tests in the past, the GRE Reading Comprehension questions should be no problem at all. If your comprehension skills are subpar, if you freeze when faced with difficult reading passages, if you read very slowly, or if English is not your first language, you should take the time to work through this section of the book.

Read

The best way to learn to read better is to read more. If you read only materials in your chosen discipline, you are limiting yourself in a way that may show up on your GRE score. Reading broadly in subject areas that do not, at first glance, hold much appeal for you will train you to focus your attention on what you are reading. Pick up a journal in a field you do not know. Read an article. Summarize the key ideas. Decide whether the author's argument makes sense to you. Think about where the author might go next with his or her argument. Finally, consider how the content of the article relates to your life or to the lives of people you know.

All of this may sound like a chore, but it is the key to making yourself read actively. An active reader interacts with a text rather than bouncing off it. Success on the GRE's Reading Comprehension questions requires active reading.

You can use any of the following strategies to focus your attention on your reading. You may use many of them already, quite automatically. Others may be just what you need to shift your reading comprehension into high gear.

Active Reading Strategies

- **Monitor Your Understanding**   When faced with a difficult text, it's all too easy to zone out and skip through challenging passages. You will not have that luxury when the text you are reading is only 150 words long and it is followed by questions that require your understanding. Pay attention to how you are feeling about a text. Are you getting the author's main points? Is there something that makes little or no sense? Are there words that you do not know? Figuring out what makes a passage hard for you is the first step toward correcting the problem. Once you figure it out, you can use one of the following strategies to improve your connection to the text.

- **Predict**   Your ability to make predictions is surprisingly important to your ability to read well. If a passage is well organized, you should be able to read the introductory sentences and have a pretty good sense of where the author is going with the text. Practice this one starting with newspaper articles, where the main ideas are supposed to appear in the first paragraph. Move on to more difficult reading. See whether your expectation of a text holds up through the reading of the text. Making predictions about what you are about to read is an immediate way to engage with the text and keep you engaged throughout your reading.

- **Ask Questions**   Keep a running dialogue with yourself as you read. You don't have to stop reading; just pause to consider: What does this mean? Why did the author use this word? Where is he or she going with this argument? Why is this important? Then answer your own questions. This will become second nature after a while. When you become acclimated to asking yourself questions as you read a test passage, you may discover that some of the questions you asked appear in different forms on the test itself.

- **Summarize** You do this when you take notes in class or when you prepare an outline as you study for an exam. Try doing it as you read unfamiliar materials, but do it in your head. At the end of a particularly dense paragraph, try to reduce the author's verbiage to a single, cogent sentence that states the main idea. At the end of a longer passage, see whether you can restate the theme or message in a phrase or two.

- **Connect** Every piece of writing is a communication between the author and the reader. You connect to a text first by bringing your prior knowledge to that text and last by applying what you learn from the text to some area of your life. Even if you know nothing at all about architecture or archaeology, your lifetime of experience in the world carries a lot of weight as you read an article about those topics. Connecting to a text can lead to "Aha!" moments as you say to yourself, "I knew that!" or even "I never knew that!" If you're barreling through a text passively, you will not give yourself time to connect. You might as well record the passage and play it under your pillow as you sleep.

Pace Yourself

You will have 30 minutes to answer the 20 or so Verbal questions in each section of the test. If you are a slow reader, you are at a decided disadvantage. It would be a shame to lose points because you failed to complete a passage or two.

You do not need to speed-read to perform well on the Reading Comprehension section, but you might benefit from some pointers that speed-readers use.

Speed-Reading Strategies

- **Avoid Subvocalizing** You probably don't move your lips while you read, but you may find yourself "saying" the text in your head. This slows you down significantly, because you are slowing down to speech speed instead of revving up to reading speed. You do not need to "say" the words; the connection between your eyes and your brain is perfectly able to bypass that step.
- **Don't Regress** If you don't understand something, you may run your eyes back and forth and back and forth over it. Speed-readers know this as "regression," and it's a big drag on reading speed. It's better to read once all the way through and then reread a section that caused you confusion.
- **Bundle Ideas** Read phrases rather than words. Remember, you are being tested on overall meaning, which is derived not from single words but rather from phrases, sentences, and paragraphs. If you read word by word, your eye stops constantly, and that slows you down.

Read bundles of meaning, and your eyes will flow over the page, improving both reading speed and comprehension.

Preview

When it comes to taking tests, knowing what to expect is half the battle. The GRE's Reading Comprehension questions assess a variety of reading skills, from the most basic comprehension skills to the higher-level application and synthesis skills. The next part of this chapter is a breakdown of skills you should expect to see tested.

READING COMPREHENSION SKILLS

You may not be tested on every one of these skills, but you will probably see a mixture of several question types on your GRE. Understanding the skills will help you prepare for the questions.

Identify the Main Idea

When you identify the main idea, you look for the most important idea in a passage or paragraph. Suppose you are reading an article and a friend asks, "What is that about?" Your answer is the main idea.

Sample Question Stems

- Which of the following best states the author's main point?
- Which of the following would be the best title for the passage?
- Which title best summarizes the main idea of the passage?

Identify the Author's Purpose

The author's purpose is related to the main idea. Identifying the author's purpose is equivalent to identifying the reason for the passage's existence—the reason a reader might read it, the reason it was written in the first place.

In addition, the author's purpose might refer to a specific phrase or example used by the author to make a specific point.

Sample Question Stems

- The author of the passage is primarily concerned with . . .
- The primary purpose of the passage is to . . .
- The author's main purpose is to . . .
- The example given in line XX is intended by the author to . . .
- The author quotes X in order to . . .
- The author mentions X in order to . . .
- The author refers to X in line XX primarily in order to . . .

Identify Supporting Details

Supporting details are those details that support the main idea. They may tell who, what, when, or how. Instead of asking "What color is the horse," questions on the GRE are more likely to ask, "According to the passage, the horse is . . ." The possible answers are likely to include details that exist in the passage but do not really answer the question.

A trickier way of testing your understanding of details is to offer a set of questions and ask you which of those questions is answered by information from the passage. This is the only kind of detail question that requires you to think outside the text. It is a form of extrapolation. (See below.)

Sample Question Stems

- According to the passage, which of these is true?
- The author states that which of the following is so?
- All of the following are mentioned in the passage *except* . . .
- Which of the following statements is accurate?
- The passage provides information to answer which of these questions?

Make Inferences/Draw Conclusions

Identifying main ideas and identifying supporting details are literal comprehension skills. This means that all the information needed to answer the question is found directly in the passage. Questions that test your ability to make inferences or drawing conclusions are different. They require you to make a leap and apply what you already know to the information found in a passage. Often, the GRE will clue you in to this type of question by using the word *infer* or *imply*.

Sample Question Stems

- You can infer from the passage that . . .
- The author implies that . . .
- The passage implies that . . .
- It can be inferred from lines XX–XX that . . .

Identify the Author's Perspective

An author's perspective is that author's attitude toward his or her subject matter. It might reveal itself through tone, through word choice, or through focus. For example, two authors writing about opera might have two very different attitudes. One might praise opera as the finest of musical art forms. The other might view it with amusement or disdain.

On the GRE, you might be asked to describe the author's attitude by choosing a particular adjective, or you might need to apply your understanding of the author's perspective to a theory or statement outside the passage itself.

Sample Question Stems

- In lines XX–XX, the author's attitude toward X could be described as . . .
- The author's attitude toward X might best be described as . . .
- The author of the passage would most likely agree that . . .
- According to the passage, the author considers X to be . . .
- With which of these statements would the author probably agree?

Analyze an Argument

Many nonfiction passages involve an argument on the part of the author. The author writes about a topic in order to make a particular point. That point is the author's argument. For example, the author might write about bird feeders to make the argument that they should be used only in the winter, because the birds have ample food sources in summer. On the GRE, you may be asked to locate a counterargument that weakens the author's argument or to choose a way to strengthen the author's existing argument. You might also be given statements from outside the passage and asked to select the one that best supports the author's theory.

Sample Question Stems

- The author's assertions about X would be weakened if . . .
- Which of the following, if true, would make the author's assertions most difficult to verify?
- Which of these findings would best support the author's hypothesis?
- The author's argument would be strengthened if . . .

Extrapolate

When you extrapolate, you infer unknown information from known information. On the GRE, this means that you take what is given in a passage and apply it to an outside example. For example, you might read a passage about the differences among pine, spruce, and fir trees and then apply what you've learned to a specific description of an unfamiliar tree.

Sample Question Stems

- Which of the following would be an example of X as described in line XX?
- The author suggests that if X were to happen, . . .
- The process described in the passage most closely resembles . . .

Analyze Structure

Every passage, even one as short as those on the GRE, has a structure. The sentences progress in a sensible order, and one thought leads logically to the next.

Questions on the GRE may require you to analyze the logic of the passage's construction or to determine which of several possible statements would most reasonably be added to the passage.

Sample Question Stems

- Lines XX and YY are logically related to each other in that . . .
- Which of these statements would be most likely to follow the last sentence of the passage?
- Which statement could most logically follow the last sentence in the passage?

Try It Yourself

Read the passage, which is longer than those you will see on the GRE. Then follow the directions. Some possible answers are given.

A land bridge is land exposed when the sea recedes, connecting one expanse of land to another. One land bridge that still exists today is the Sinai Peninsula, which attaches the Middle East to North Africa. Central America is another land bridge, this one connecting North to South America.

Historical land bridges are many. There was a bridge connecting the British Isles to the European continent, and there was one between Spain and Morocco at what is now the Strait of Gibraltar. There were bridges connecting Japan to China and Korea. One of the most famous land bridges was the Bering Land Bridge, often known as Beringia, which connected Alaska to Siberia across what is now the Bering Strait.

The Bering Land Bridge was not terribly long. If it still existed today, you could drive it in your car in about an hour. It appeared during the Ice Age, when enormous sheets of ice covered much of Europe and America. The ice sheets contained huge amounts of water north of the equator, and because of this, the sea level dropped precipitously, perhaps as much as 400 feet, revealing landmasses such as the Bering Land Bridge.

At this time, the ecology of the northern hemisphere was that of the Mammoth Steppe. It was a dry, frigid land filled with grasses, sedges, and tundra vegetation. It supported many large, grazing animals including reindeer, bison, and muskoxen, as well as the lions that fed upon them. It also contained large camels, giant short-faced bears, and woolly mammoths.

The Bering Land Bridge may have been somewhat wetter than other areas of the Mammoth Steppe, since it was bordered north and south by ocean and fed by ocean breezes. Many of the animals of the Mammoth Steppe used the bridge to cross from east to west and back again. Eventually, their human hunters tracked them from Asia to North America.

Ethnologists and geologists generally believe that humans used the Bering Land Bridge to populate the Americas, which up until about 24,000 years ago had no sign of human life. Ethnologists use evidence such as shared religions, similar houses and tools, and unique methods of cleaning and preserving food to show the link between the people of coastal Siberia and the people of coastal Alaska.

1. Give the passage a title that expresses its main idea.

2. Name two existing land bridges and two historical land bridges.

Existing Land Bridges	Historical Land Bridges

3. Based on the information in the article, estimate the length of the Bering Land Bridge.

   About _____ miles

4. What two reasons does the author give to support her notion that the Bering Land Bridge may have been wetter than other areas of the Mammoth Steppe? Underline them.

5. Based on the passage, which of these would be considered a land bridge? (Use an atlas if you need one.) Why?

   Strait of Hormuz   yes   no   _____

   Isthmus of Panama   yes   no   _____

   Khyber Pass   yes   no   _____

Answers and Explanations

1. Possible answers might be: "Land Bridges" or "The Bering Land Bridge." (*Main Idea*)

2. Existing: Sinai Peninsula, Central America; Historical: connecting the British Isles to the European continent, connecting Spain to Morocco, connecting Japan to China and Korea, Bering Land Bridge. (*Supporting Details*)

3. Anywhere from 40 to 70 miles, based on the fact that "you could drive it . . . in about an hour." (*Make Inferences*)

4. Bordered north and south by oceans; fed by ocean breezes. (*Analyze Argument*)

5. Strait of Hormuz, no—it is entirely water; Isthmus of Panama, yes— it is a strip of land that connects one expanse to another; Khyber Pass, no—it does not fit the definition. (*Extrapolate*)

CHAPTER 6

SENTENCE STRUCTURE

CHAPTER GOALS

- Identify the eight parts of speech.
- Use context clues to determine the part of speech and likely meaning of an unfamiliar word.
- Recognize signal words and the relationships they indicate.

Understanding grammar and sentence structure will help you with Text Completions and Sentence Equivalences on the GRE. You may not have conducted a real study of grammar since middle school. Even if that is true, a quick review may be all you need.

PARTS OF SPEECH

On the GRE, all Text Completion and Sentence Equivalence questions require you to determine which word or words best complete a given sentence or passage. To do that, you need to have some understanding of sentence structure and the way words are used to construct meaning.

We use the eight parts of speech as the building blocks of our sentences. The order in which we use them affects the meaning of those sentences. For example, "All bears sleep in caves" means something different from "All bears in caves sleep."

Here are the eight parts of speech.

Nouns

A noun names a person, place, thing, or idea. Nouns come in singular and plural forms. In other languages, nouns may have gender, too.

	Person	Place	Thing	Idea
Singular	man, firefighter	city, planet	truck, table	kindness, faith
Plural	men, firefighters	cities, planets	trucks, tables	kindnesses, faiths

Nouns come in two classes: common and proper. A proper noun names a particular person, place, thing, or (occasionally) idea. It always begins with a capital letter.

Proper	Judith, Dr. Chao	Spain, Lake Erie	Volvo, *Titanic*

Pronouns

A pronoun is used to take the place of a noun or nouns. For example, in the sentence "Jessica said she preferred Chinese food," *she* is a pronoun that takes the place of repeating the word *Jessica*.

The most commonly used pronouns are those we call *personal pronouns*.

	First Person	Second Person	Third Person
Singular	I, me, my, mine	you, your, yours	he, him, his, she, her, hers, it, its
Plural	we, us, our, ours	you, your, yours	they, them, their, theirs

Personal pronouns may be extended to form reflexive pronouns.

	First Person	Second Person	Third Person
Singular	myself	yourself	himself, herself, itself
Plural	ourselves	yourselves	themselves

Interrogative pronouns are used to begin questions.

Who   Whose   Whom   What   Which

Demonstrative pronouns are used in place of nouns. They point out a particular person, place, or thing. The same words may be used as adjectives.

this   that   these   those

Pronoun: <u>This</u> is a wonderful book.

Adjective: I just love <u>this</u> book.

Indefinite pronouns do not name a particular person or thing. Some are singular, and some are plural. Others may be used either way.

Singular	anybody, anyone, each, either, everybody, everyone, neither, nobody, no one, one, somebody, someone
Plural	both, few, many, several
Depends on Context	any, all, most, none, some

Verbs

A verb expresses action or a state of being. A noun or pronoun plus a verb can equal a sentence. True, it isn't a very interesting sentence, but it's a sentence nevertheless.

> Anita sang.   Ducks dive.   I wonder.

Action verbs express action. An action verb is transitive when its action is directed toward a person or thing named in the sentence.

- Anita <u>sang</u> a song. (Anita's action, *singing,* is directed toward *song.*)

A verb is intransitive when its action has no object.

- Ducks <u>dive</u> downward. (The ducks are diving, but there is no receiver of that action.)

Helping verbs are added to other verbs to form verb phrases.

- I <u>had been wondering</u> about that.
- Grace <u>may have finished</u> the book.

Linking verbs connect one noun or pronoun to another word in the sentence. The other word renames or describes the noun or pronoun. Many linking verbs are forms of the verb *to be.*

- I <u>am</u> a writer. (The word *I* is linked to *writer.*)
- Daniel <u>should have been</u> exhausted. (The word *Daniel* is linked to *ex-hausted.*)

The time expressed by a verb is called its *tense.* Every verb has six tenses in English. Here are the singular first-person tenses of the regular verb *to explore.*

Present	Past	Future	Present Perfect	Past Perfect	Future Perfect
I explore	I explored	I will explore	I have explored	I had explored	I will have explored

Adjectives

An adjective describes, or modifies, a noun or pronoun. Adjectives can tell what kind, which one, or how many. They usually appear just before the word they modify, but they may also follow a linking verb.

- I enjoyed the <u>mocha</u> ice cream. (*Mocha* tells what kind of ice cream.)
- Do you like <u>that</u> jacket? (*That* tells which jacket is meant.)
- <u>Twelve</u> posts held up the fence. (*Twelve* tells how many posts.)
- Kate was <u>pleased</u> by the attention. (*Pleased* modifies *Kate* and follows a linking verb.)

Articles are adjectives, too. *A* and *an* are indefinite articles—they refer to one member of a general group.

- <u>A</u> child rode by on *a* bicycle.
- <u>An</u> onion can add flavor to *a* stew.

The is a definite article that refers to a particular place or thing.

- <u>The</u> child rode by on a bicycle. (The child is someone specific.)
- An onion might add flavor to <u>the</u> stew. (The stew is one that is particularly meant.)

Adverbs

An adverb modifies a verb, an adjective, or another adverb. When it modifies a verb, an adverb may tell where, when, how, or to what extent. It may appear before or after the verb, or it may even divide a verb phrase.

- Come <u>here</u>. (*Here* tells where to come.)
- We will talk <u>later</u>. (*Later* tells when we will talk.)
- <u>Loudly</u>, they laughed. (*Loudly* tells how they laughed.)
- I will <u>never</u> forgive him. (*Never* tells to what extent I will forgive.)

When adverbs modify adjectives, they typically tell to what extent.

- She seems <u>completely</u> calm. (*Completely* tells to what extent she seems calm.)

- I was <u>rather</u> surprised. (*Rather* tells to what extent I was surprised.)

Certain adverbs may also be used to tell to what extent about other adverbs in a sentence.

- Joanne is <u>almost</u> always punctual. (*Almost* modifies the adverb *always.*)
- We called them <u>much</u> earlier. (*Much* modifies the adverb *earlier.*)

Prepositions

A preposition relates a noun or pronoun to another word in the sentence. Different prepositions create different meanings.

- The horse stood <u>beside</u> the barn.
- The horse stood <u>behind</u> the barn.
- The horse stood <u>inside</u> the barn.
- We will meet <u>after</u> lunch.
- We will meet <u>during</u> lunch.
- We will meet <u>for</u> lunch.

A prepositional phrase begins with a preposition and ends with a noun or pronoun. *Beside the barn* and *during lunch* are examples of prepositional phrases.

Conjunctions

A conjunction connects words or groups of words in a sentence. There are three kinds of conjunctions. Coordinating conjunctions join items of the same kind, whether those are nouns, prepositional phrases, or clauses.

- My favorite books are by Jane Austen <u>and</u> Charles Dickens. (joining two nouns)
- We can work for Senator McCall <u>or</u> for Governor Dean. (joining two prepositional phrases)
- She enjoys opera, <u>but</u> she likes Broadway musicals better. (joining two independent clauses)

Correlative conjunctions serve the same purpose, but they are always used in pairs.

- <u>Both</u> Sandy <u>and</u> Max are undergraduates. (joining two nouns)
- He asked <u>not only</u> for pizza <u>but also</u> for cake. (joining two prepositional phrases)
- <u>Either</u> Mollie will graduate early, <u>or</u> she will transfer to a cheaper school. (joining two independent clauses)

Subordinating conjunctions introduce adverb clauses, which are parts of a sentence that modify a verb, an adjective, or an adverb.

- <u>After</u> I finish my work, I will go for a walk in the botanical garden.
- Hector cannot graduate <u>because</u> he owes the library some money.
- <u>Unless</u> you have some objection, Dr. Morton will examine you.

The words in the following chart are typically used as subordinating conjunctions. Note that some of them may be used as prepositions as well.

after	although	as	as if	as long as	as soon as
because	before	if	in order that	now that	rather than
since	so that	than	though	unless	until
when	whenever	where	whereas	wherever	while

Interjections

An interjection is an exclamatory word that is used to express strong feeling. Unlike other parts of speech, interjections have no relation to the sentence as a whole.

- <u>Well</u>, I knew that would never work.
- <u>Wow!</u> The concert was terrific!
- <u>Oh, no!</u> Someone scratched my car!

Try It Yourself

Write the part of speech of each underlined word in the following list. Write *noun, pronoun, verb, adjective, adverb, preposition, conjunction,* or *interjection*. Answers appear following the list.

1. Please turn the light <u>off</u>.   _____

2. <u>That</u> was an unusual show.   _____

3. <u>Gee</u>, I wonder who called?   _____

4. Look <u>into</u> this telescope.   _____

5. We studied <u>microbiology</u>.   _____

6. <u>Did</u> you <u>order</u> lunch yet?   _____

7. Gwen <u>and</u> I saw the movie.   _____

8. His lecture was <u>tedious</u>.   _____

9. Vinh <u>captured</u> a tiny mouse. _____

10. Do your <u>daily</u> exercises.   _____

11. <u>Hey</u>! Don't forget to write!   _____

12. <u>Either</u> he <u>or</u> I will win.   _____

13. Wait <u>under</u> the overhang.   _____

14. Let's meet <u>later</u> to chat.   _____

15. <u>Everyone</u> enjoyed the feast. _____

16. Does he envy our <u>freedom</u>?   _____

Answers and Explanations

1. *Off* is an adverb that tells how to turn the light.

2. *That* is a demonstrative pronoun.

3. Interjection.

4. Preposition.

5. Noun.

6. *Did order* is a verb phrase.

7. Conjunction.

8. *Tedious* is an adjective modifying *lecture*.

9. Verb.

10. In this sentence, *daily* is an adjective modifying *exercises*.

11. Interjection.

12. *Either/or* is a correlative conjunction.

13. Preposition.

14. *Later* is an adverb that tells when to meet.

15. *Everyone* is an indefinite pronoun.

16. *Freedom* is a noun that names an idea.

CONTEXT CLUES

As you read, you can use the words and sentences that surround an unfamiliar word to determine that word's part of speech and definition. This is a skill you use unconsciously as you read; otherwise, you would rarely get through a text without continually consulting a dictionary.

Your knowledge of English grammar can help you use context clues. For example, here is a cloze sentence (a sentence with a word omitted). Text Completion and Sentence Equivalence questions on the GRE use just this format.

The _____ grasped a branch and held on.

Any speaker of English quickly understands that the missing word must be a noun. Only a noun or pronoun can perform the action of a verb such as *grasped*. Only a noun can be introduced by the article *the*.

The gibbon grasped a branch and held on.

Even if you don't know the meaning of *gibbon,* you may know enough just by understanding that it is a noun that names something that can grasp and hold onto a branch. It clearly is not a type of building or planet; its exact definition may elude you, but you know a lot about what it is by eliminating what it cannot be.

Hooting at the tourists who peered into its cage, the gibbon grasped a branch and held on.

As you can see, adding more context clues helps you determine specific meaning.

Here is another example.

He was awakened by the _____ sound.

The word must be an adjective that tells what kind of sound awakened him.

He was awakened by the cacophonous sound.
He was awakened by the cacophonous sound of seven taxis fighting over a single lane.

The final sentence has enough context clues to alert you to the meaning of the word *cacophonous*.

Try It Yourself

For each blank, consider what part of speech the missing word must be. Then write a possible word to complete each sentence. Possible answers appear after the exercise.

1. Shakespeare wrote a number of _____ that describe the power of love over time.

2. Professor Kinsley gave a fine speech _____ Kulp Auditorium last Saturday night.

3. Anyone can learn to read music, _____ very few people have perfect pitch.

4. _____! The dumpster outside the kitchen smells absolutely disgusting!

5. From their room in the dormitory tower, we _____ the entire countryside.

6. Dorothy worked _____ to get her grades up after her long illness.

7. Please give my wallet back to _____; I worked hard for that money.

8. A _____ bird trilled prettily from the bush outside the library window.

Answers and Explanations

1. The word must be a noun. Possible answers include *poems* or *sonnets*.

2. The word must be a preposition. Possible answers include *at, in,* or *about.*

3. The word must be a conjunction. The best answer is probably *but.*

4. The word must be an interjection. Possible answers include *Phew* or *Ugh.*

5. The word must be a verb. Possible answers include *could see* or *surveyed*.

6. The word must be an adverb. Possible answers include *hard* or *diligently*.

7. The word must be a pronoun or noun. The best answer is probably *me*.

8. The word must be an adjective. Possible answers include *tiny* or *colorful*.

SIGNAL WORDS

Certain words in a sentence determine the relationship between or among ideas. Often, these words are adverbs, prepositions, or conjunctions. As you take the GRE, you will come across Text Completion or Sentence Equivalence questions that use these signal words. Understanding the relationships created by these words will help you solve these types of questions.

- Jackie is disorganized; <u>moreover</u>, she cannot be trusted. (The second clause is a continuation of or addition to the first.)

- Jackie is disorganized; <u>therefore</u>, she is a poor choice to manage the project. (The second clause is a conclusion based on the first.)

- Jackie is disorganized; <u>similarly</u>, Cleo is something of a slob. (The second clause compares to the first.)

- Jackie is disorganized, <u>but</u> Greg is quite systematic. (The second clause contrasts with the first.)

- Jackie is disorganized <u>due to</u> her stressful home life. (The final phrase provides evidence or reasons to support the first clause.)

Here are some words and phrases that may be used as signals in sentences.

Continuation/Addition	additionally, besides, furthermore, in addition, moreover
Conclusion	consequently, hence, in other words, so, therefore, thus
Comparison	as well, both/and, equally, just as, like, likewise, similarly, too
Contrast	although, but, despite, however, nevertheless, whereas
Evidence/Reasons	as a result, because, due to, for that reason, given that, since

Try It Yourself

Complete each sentence using a clause or phrase that makes sense in context. Use the signal words to help you. Possible answers are given following the sentences.

1. Pepper adds flavor to bland dishes; furthermore, _____.

2. I always treated my grandfather kindly; as a result, _____.

3. Although he really could not sing very well, Jack _____.

4. Just as parakeets make friendly pets, _____.

5. The roads seemed unusually icy, so _____.

6. Besides looking beautiful in her gown, _____.

7. Darnell speaks French very well; however, _____.

8. Because wild animals may carry diseases, _____.

9. Both kings and emperors _____.

10. First graders are just learning to read; therefore, _____.

Answers and Explanations

1. *Furthermore* indicates an additional thought or a continuation of the existing thought. A possible sentence might be: "Pepper adds flavor to bland dishes; furthermore, it can add a dash of color."

2. *As a result* indicates a reason. A possible sentence might be: "I always treated my grandfather kindly; as a result, he left me a nice inheritance."

3. *Although* indicates contrast. A possible sentence might be: "Although he really could not sing very well, Jack enjoyed participating in the community chorus."

4. *Just as* indicates a comparison. A possible sentence might be: "Just as parakeets make friendly pets, so do their larger cousins, the parrots."

5. *So* indicates a conclusion. A possible sentence might be: "The roads seemed unusually icy, so Mr. Dobbs drove slowly."

6. *Besides* indicates a continuation or addition. A possible sentence might be: "Besides looking beautiful in her gown, the bride had a radiant smile."

7. *However* indicates a contrast. A possible sentence might be: "Darnell speaks French very well; however, his Russian is difficult to understand."

8. *Because* indicates a reason. A possible sentence might be: "Because wild animals may carry diseases, it is a bad idea to welcome one into your home."

9. *Both/and* indicates a comparison. A possible sentence might be: "Both kings and emperors rule over tracts of land."

10. *Therefore* indicates a conclusion. A possible sentence might be: "First graders are just learning to read; therefore, their textbooks contain few words and many pictures."

SENTENCE STRUCTURE DRILL

Identify the part of speech of each underlined word in these sentences from the Declaration of Independence. Write *noun, pronoun, verb, adjective, adverb, preposition, conjunction,* or *interjection.* Answers appear at the end of the drill.

We (1) hold these truths to be self-evident, that (2) all men are created equal, that (3) they are endowed (4) by their Creator with certain unalienable Rights, that among these are Life, Liberty and the pursuit of (5) Happiness.

And for (6) the support of this Declaration, (7) with a firm (8) reliance on the Protection of Divine Providence, we (9) mutually pledge to each other our Lives, our Fortunes (10) and our Sacred Honor.

1. _____

2. _____

3. _____

4. _____

5. _____

6. _____

7. _____

8. _____

9. _____

10. _____

Use the word *whereas* in a sentence that shows contrast.

11. _____

Use the word *similarly* in a sentence that shows comparison.

12. _____

Answers and Explanations

1. Verb.

2. Adjective (modifying *men*).

3. Pronoun (replacing *men*).

4. Preposition.

5. Noun.

6. Adjective (article).

7. Preposition.

8. Noun.

9. Adverb (modifying *pledge*).

10. Conjunction.

11. Possible sentence: Whereas I always read before bedtime, my roommate likes to watch TV instead.

12. Possible sentence: Koalas are considered cuddly animals; similarly, pandas have a congenial reputation.

PART III
ITEM FORMATS AND SOLUTION STRATEGIES

CHAPTER 7

GRE SENTENCE EQUIVALENCE QUESTIONS

CHAPTER GOALS

• Study examples of Sentence Equivalence questions.

• Learn specific strategies for answering Sentence Equivalence questions.

• Practice answering sample GRE Sentence Equivalence questions.

Sentence Equivalence questions test a variety of language skills. They require you to complete a sentence with a pair of synonyms selected from a list of six possible choices. Not only must you find answers that create a meaningful sentence, but you must also select two different answers that give the sentence an identical meaning.

ITEM FORMAT: GRE SENTENCE EQUIVALENCE

Unlike the other types of questions in Verbal Reasoning, Sentence Equivalence questions have only one consistent format:

Select *two* answer choices that (1) complete the sentence in a way that makes sense and (2) produce sentences that are similar in meaning.

Because he had studied so hard and knew the material backward and forward, Cal could afford to be _____ about his chances on the final exam.

- A. edgy
- B. dyspeptic
- C. optimistic
- D. facile
- E. sanguine
- F. benevolent

In this example, the word *because* sets up a cause-and-effect relationship between the parts of the sentence. Think: Cal has studied hard and knows the material; therefore, he feels X. He would not feel *edgy* (choice A) or *dyspeptic* (choice B) if he really knew the material. He might feel *optimistic* (choice C). A good synonym for *optimistic* is *sanguine* (choice E). So selecting choice C and choice E gives you two sentences that make sense and are essentially identical in meaning.

> **FORMAT TIP**
>
> It's easy to lose points on the GRE by forgetting that all Sentence Equivalence questions require two answers, not just one. You get no partial credit for making one selection—or for selecting one correct and one incorrect response.

Note that it is not enough simply to skim the answer choices and pick out the synonyms. There may be two sets of synonyms among the answer choices, but only one set will fit the context and build a logical sentence.

SOLUTION STRATEGIES: GRE SENTENCE EQUIVALENCE

Many of the skills from Chapter 6 will help you as you answer Sentence Equivalence questions. In particular, review the section entitled "Context Clues" (pages 74–76). Although there are many ways to attack a Sentence Equivalence question, what follows is a simple strategy that will help you remember to select two responses.

Identify Synonyms

Synonyms are words with identical or similar meanings. A thesaurus is essentially a book of synonyms. Here are a couple of typical thesaurus entries:

> **invariable** *adj.* unvarying, constant, steady; uniform, fixed; monotonous; permanent. SEE STABILITY, REGULARITY, PERMANENCE.
> **invasion** *n.* infringement, encroachment, violation; raid, foray, ATTACK. SEE WARFARE.

Note that not every synonym makes sense in every sentence. There are shades of meaning among synonyms that may be quite subtle. For example, an invasion of privacy might be referred to as a "violation," but it would never be called a "foray."

You may wish to begin your approach to a Sentence Equivalence question by identifying the synonyms in the set of six answer choices. As noted, this will not necessarily ensure that you know the answer; you must still plug your answers into the sentence to check them against the context.

> **FORMAT TIP**
>
> In any given list of six word choices, there may be words you do not know. Don't get bogged down in trying to recall the meanings of those words—they may not even be the answers you seek. On the other hand, if you end up finding one answer that clearly fits, four choices that do not fit, and one unknown word, you can feel fairly confident that the unknown word is your second answer.

Try It Yourself

Circle two synonyms in each set of six words.

1.	boisterous	tedious	animated	tranquil	politic	noisome
2.	calumny	approach	tactic	vicinity	episode	prologue
3.	appetite	rejection	scrutiny	diversion	analysis	aftermath
4.	marginal	droll	conclusive	sporadic	tangential	imperative
5.	recurrent	scathing	brilliant	ultimate	exotic	alien
6.	depleted	incompetent	unskilled	adept	disingenuous	forthright
7.	intuitive	transient	composed	discerning	perturbed	mordant
8.	resolve	deflect	agitate	engross	retain	involve
9.	inquisition	prodigy	hazard	examination	invective	dilemma
10.	endeavor	conspire	dispute	controvert	dissect	alleviate

Write a synonym for each of these words, which are taken from the vocabulary list in Chapter 4. Check your work by referring to the list or to a thesaurus.

11. avarice   _____

12. cajole   _____

13. edict   _____

14. germane   _____

15. inimitable   _____

16. kismet   _____

17. meander   _____

18. odious   _____

19. ribald   _____

20. turbid   _____

Answers and Explanations

1. *Boisterous* and *animated* refer to a kind of noisy energy. *Noisome* means smelly, not noisy.

2. An *approach* to a problem is the same as a *tactic.* Remember to think about all possible meanings of a word before making a choice.

3. *Scrutiny* and *analysis* refer to a careful inspection of something. Look up the other words if they are unfamiliar to you.

4. If something is *marginal,* meaning "minor" or "unimportant," it is *tangential.*

5. Something that is *exotic,* or foreign and unfamiliar, may be called *alien.*

6. If you are *incompetent,* or not competent, you are *unskilled,* or not skilled. Notice that an antonym, *adept,* is thrown in to confuse you.

7. A person who is *intuitive* may be said to be *discerning*—not in the sense of being discriminating in taste, but rather in the sense of being perceptive. Again, consider all possible meanings of the words that you are given.

8. If something *engrosses* you, it *involves* you, whether it is a difficult problem or an exciting story.

9. We think of the capital I–Inquisition when we see this word, but an *inquisition* is simply an *examination.*

10. If you *dispute* a point, you may *controvert,* or contradict, it.

11. Possible answers include *greed, cupidity, materialism.*

12. Possible answers include *coax, persuade, wheedle.*

13. Possible answers include *proclamation, announcement, decree.*

14. Possible answers include *relevant, pertinent, applicable.*

15. Possible answers include *unique, unmatched, incomparable.*

16. Possible answers include *fate, luck, destiny.*

17. Possible answers include *wander, ramble, wind.*

18. Possible answers include *hateful, abhorrent, loathsome.*

19. Possible answers include *coarse, vulgar, bawdy.*

20. Possible answers include *cloudy, murky, muddy.*

Use Context Clues

Once you've identified synonyms, you still need to see whether those words fit the context of the sentence. You can begin by reading the sentence and imagining a word that completes it and makes sense:

Teresa is impossible to dislike; her _____ attitude brightens everyone's day.

There are two main clues in this sentence. The first is "impossible to dislike," which indicates that any word that describes Teresa's attitude will be positive in connotation. The second is "brightens everyone's day," which implies a particular sort of attitude that has an upbeat impact. Given those clues, you can tell that words such as *melancholy* or *unpleasant*—although they fit the sentence syntactically, being the right parts of speech—fail to fit the sentence semantically, because they do not support the meaning.

You can imagine the sorts of words that *would* fit and be logical:

Teresa is impossible to dislike; her *sunny* attitude brightens everyone's day.

Teresa is impossible to dislike; her *cheerful* attitude brightens everyone's day.

Teresa is impossible to dislike; her *convivial* attitude brightens everyone's day.

Once you have determined the sort of word that fits the semantics of the sentence, it's just a matter of finding two of that sort of word among the choices you are given.

Try It Yourself

Finish each sentence with a word that makes sense syntactically and semantically.

1. Unless he improves his _____, James will have a difficult time in graduate school.

2. Ally failed to _____ our warning and therefore missed the turn-off to the motel.

3. Because he received the writing award, we expected Hiro to write with _____.

4. Don't trust her _____ smile; she has always hidden her deceit behind a mask.

5. Although Marta had a good, solid job, she often still felt _____ about her future.

Answers and Explanations

1. The answer must be a noun that has something to do with success in graduate school; possible answers are *grades, attitude, writing, English,* and so on.

2. The answer must be a verb that can have *warning* as its direct object; possible answers are *heed, hear, accept, trust,* and so on.

3. The answer must be a noun that applies to the writing of an award-winning writer; possible answers are *panache, flair, ease, confidence,* and so on.

4. The answer must be an adjective that describes the smile of a deceitful person; possible answers are *fraudulent, false, cunning, unctuous,* and so on.

5. The answer must be an adjective that describes a woman who isn't entirely satisfied with her good, solid job (as evidenced by the clue word *although*); possible answers are *uneasy, anxious, ambivalent, insecure,* and so on.

Use the Process of Elimination

You may use the process of elimination anytime you face a multiple-choice test, but it is especially useful here. Immediately eliminate any of the answer choices that simply do not fit the context of the sentence. Next, eliminate any choices that have no synonyms. You will be left with the correct response.

Unless he improves his _____, James will have a difficult time in graduate school.

A	grades	→	*This makes sense in context but has no synonym.*
B	attitude	→	*This fits the context. Does it have a synonym in the list?*
C	writing	→	*This fits the context but has no synonym.*
D	correlation	→	*This does not make much sense in context.*
E	(outlook)	→	*This fits and is a synonym for attitude.*
F	hypothesis	→	*This does not fit the sentence.*

SENTENCE EQUIVALENCE DRILL 1

Select *two* answer choices that (1) complete the sentence in a way that makes sense and (2) produce sentences that are similar in meaning. Answers appear at the end of the drill sets.

1. The World Cup took place on the continent of Africa for the very first time in 2010; _____ were high for an exciting and well-attended event.

　A emotions

　B expectations

　C interests

　D athletes

　E adventures

　F prospects

2. Everyone has heard of the poet John Milton, but few realize that his father, also John Milton, was an _____ composer.

　A admired

　B erstwhile

　C established

　D esteemed

　E accepted

　F affluent

3. Unless you have traveled _____ in Northumberland, England, you have probably never been to the tiny village of Swarland.

　A exclusively

　B repeatedly

　C intricately

　D extensively

　E recently

　F widely

4. Although most land snails are _____, the giant African snail is a notable exception; it can be 15 inches long and weigh 2 pounds.

   A gargantuan

   B juvenile

   C functional

   D diminutive

   E responsive

   F minuscule

5. The Profile in Courage Award is given to individuals who risk their lives or _____ in pursuit of the public good.

   A lineage

   B careers

   C fellowship

   D livelihoods

   E identities

   F achievements

6. Beatified by the Catholic Church in 1765, Italian cleric Ludovico Sabbatini is _____ each year on the day of his death, June 11.

   A pledged

   B evoked

   C deified

   D venerated

   E honored

   F christened

7. Despite the fact that the Ozarks of Missouri and Arkansas are _____ mountains, the region is in fact a high plateau.

   A lofty

   B technically

   C reportedly

   D akin to

   E labeled

   F dubbed

8. The so-called Superfund _____ two kinds of actions: emergency removal of hazardous materials and long-term remediation of pollution and toxic substances.

   A authorizes
   B depicts
   C sanctions
   D prohibits
   E prefigures
   F assigns

9. Nanoscience is the study of very small things; the word *nano* _____ from the Greek word for "dwarf."

   A precedes
   B stems
   C relays
   D links
   E extends
   F derives

10. After Charlie Ebbets _____ its construction by selling his shares in the team, Ebbets Field formally opened in 1913.

   A enabled
   B curtailed
   C bankrolled
   D hastened
   E financed
   F ordered

▬ SENTENCE EQUIVALENCE DRILL 2

Select *two* answer choices that (1) complete the sentence in a way that makes sense and (2) produce sentences that are similar in meaning. Answers appear at the end of the drill sets.

1. Very little is known about the _____ known as Eskayan, and there are currently no native speakers of that unusual tongue.

   A dialect

   B culture

   C clan

   D island

   E atoll   *tongue*

   F language

2. In what was only Rafer Johnson's fourth competition, he _____ the existing world record in the decathlon.

   A progressed

   B valued

   C surpassed

   D prized

   E acknowledged

   F outstripped

3. Following the Treaty of Roskilde in 1658, Kronoberg Castle in Sweden lost its importance as a military structure and fell into _____.

   A shambles

   B disuse

   C setback

   D neglect

   E distress

   F siege

4. Although his original mission was a failure, Russian botanist Michael Friedrich Adams achieved an unexpected _____ when he found, by chance, the carcass of a woolly mammoth.

   A conclusion

   B upheaval

   C triumph

   D bombshell

   E success

   F venture

5. The Chicago journal known as *Poetry* has been the launching pad for many poets since its _____ in 1913; among them, T. S. Eliot, Gwendolyn Brooks, and John Ashbery.

   A extraction

   B foundation

   C partnership

   D employment

   E revival

   F inception

6. Because free hydrogen does not exist in nature, it cannot be _____ a primary energy source, as coal or oil can.

   A borne in mind

   B taken into account

   C concerned with

   D considered

   E remarked upon

   F thought of as

7. The phrase "bread and circuses" refers to early Roman politicians' plans to _____ the votes of the poor by handing out cheap food and entertainment.

   A belie

   B surmount

   C secure

   D control

   E cherish

   F earn

8. Pseudonyms are used for a variety of reasons, mostly _____; for example, to deny an actor's ethnicity, to conceal an author's gender, or to hide a revolutionary's true identity.

   [A] covert

   [B] explicit

   [C] clandestine

   [D] counterfeit

   [E] surreal

   [F] migratory

9. After the Spanish conquest of South America, Catholic priests fought against "pagan" rituals, and as a result, the popular use of hallucinogenic plants was largely _____.

   [A] engaged

   [B] endorsed

   [C] remediated

   [D] associated

   [E] suppressed

   [F] restricted

10. Frederick Law Olmsted's design of New York's Central Park was _____ in part by the designer's visit to England's Derby Arboretum in 1859.

   [A] facilitated

   [B] inspired

   [C] conceived

   [D] accelerated

   [E] influenced

   [F] structured

Answers and Explanations
Sentence Equivalence Drill 1

1. **B, F.** Although *emotions* (choice A) and *interests* (choice C) could be high (as could *athletes* [choice D], presumably), none of those three has a synonym on the list, and none works as well as *expectations* (choice B) or *prospects* (choice F).

2. **A, D.** Here, any of the answers might fit the context, but only *admired* (choice A) and *esteemed* (choice D) are synonyms that give you two sentences that are similar in meaning.

3. **D, F.** The word *unless* sets up a contrast—you probably have not seen this tiny village unless you have traveled *extensively* (choice D) or *widely* (choice F). The intimation is that the village is so small that it requires a broad range of travel even to locate it.

4. **D, F.** Here, the word *although* creates the contrast. The giant African snail is an exception to the rule for most land snails, meaning that most land snails must be small. The words that fit here are *diminutive* (choice D) and *minuscule* (choice F).

5. **B, D.** You can't easily risk your *lineage* (choice A) or *fellowship* (choice C); moreover, the only words with similar meanings on the list are *careers* (choice B) and *livelihoods* (choice D).

6. **D, E.** The cleric may be *evoked* (choice B) each year, but there is no synonym for that on the list. He has been beatified, or declared a saint, and in Catholicism, there is no way he would be *deified* (choice C), or declared a god. It is most likely that he is *venerated* (choice D) or *honored* (choice E) annually.

7. **E, F.** The Ozarks cannot be *technically* (choice B) mountains if they are in fact a high plateau. The words *despite the fact* set up a contrast that is fulfilled by the words *labeled* (choice E) and *dubbed* (choice F). They are called mountains, but they're really a plateau.

8. **A, C.** Several of the words might fit the context, but only *authorizes* (choice A) and *sanctions* (choice C) are synonyms and are syntactically logical.

9. **B, F.** *Relays* (choice C) and *extends* (choice E) are close, but the best and most accurate answers are *stems* (choice B) and *derives* (choice F).

10. **C, E.** Ebbets obviously *enabled* (choice A) the field's construction, and he may well have both *hastened* (choice D) and *ordered* (choice F) it, but the only synonym pair here is *bankrolled* (choice C) and *financed* (choice E).

Sentence Equivalence Drill 2

1. **A, F.** Eskayan could refer to a *culture* (choice B), a *clan* (choice C), an *island* (choice D), or an *atoll* (choice E) were it not for the part of the sentence that redefines the missing word by calling it "that unusual tongue." The synonyms for *tongue* are *dialect* (choice A) and *language* (choice F).

2. **C, F.** Try filling in the blank without looking at the answers. Your answer is likely to be that Rafer Johnson broke the record or beat the record. The only words on the list that fit that meaning are *surpassed* (choice C) and *outstripped* (choice F).

3. **B, D.** The castle might have fallen into a *shambles* (choice A) or perhaps into *distress* (choice E), but the only synonyms and the better responses are *disuse* (choice B) and *neglect* (choice D).

4. **C, E.** Again, the word *although* sets up a contrast; the word you are looking for will contrast with *failure*. Appropriate antonyms for *failure* include *triumph* (choice C) and *success* (choice E).

5. **B, F.** It is certainly possible that the journal was *revived* (choice E) in 1913; but only *foundation* (choice B) and *inception* (choice F) are close in meaning.

6. **D, F.** You can fill in the blanks easily if you read the sentence aloud with the choices in place. Only choices C, D, and F fit syntactically, and of those, only *considered* (choice D) and *thought of as* (choice F) are synonyms and a good semantic fit.

7. **C, F.** The politicians hoped to win votes by offering food and entertainment; the best choices, therefore, are *secure* (choice C) and *earn* (choice F).

8. **A, C.** Look at the examples in the second half of the sentence to understand the meaning of the first half of the sentence. All three examples show that pseudonyms are used to conceal identity; therefore, they have *covert* (choice A) or *clandestine* (choice C) purposes.

9. **E, F.** Think about the order of events—priests fought against rituals, which led to something happening to the popular use of hallucinogens. The most likely choices are that the use of hallucinogens was *suppressed* (choice E) or *restricted* (choice F).

10. **B, E.** A few of the choices are possible in context, but the ones that lead to similar meanings are *inspired* (choice B) and *influenced* (choice E).

CHAPTER 8

GRE TEXT COMPLETION QUESTIONS

CHAPTER GOALS

- Study examples of Text Completion questions.

- Learn specific strategies for answering Text Completion questions.

- Practice answering sample GRE Text Completion questions.

Text Completion questions are designed to test your overall understanding of the English language. Not only do they assess your knowledge of basic vocabulary, but they also assess your grasp of the grammar, or logic, of English sentences. It may seem hard to believe that filling in a blank in a sentence can test these skills, but cloze tests like this have been used since the 1950s both to test students' understanding and to evaluate the difficulty of reading passages.

ITEM FORMAT: GRE TEXT COMPLETIONS

Text Completion questions on the GRE will appear in one of the following three formats, depending on how many blanks appear in the passage given.

Complete the text by picking the best entry for each blank from the corresponding column of choices.

Although people in the Middle Ages did wash from time to time, only the wealthy could _____ to heat water for a bath.

(A)	intend
(B)	prepare
(C)	dominate
(D)	afford
(E)	ensure

Because his valise was so (i) _____, Jason found he had to stop at regular intervals to (ii) _____ his arms and back.

Blank (i)	Blank (ii)
(A) cumbersome	(D) improve
(B) tedious	(E) relieve
(C) fragile	(F) aggravate

The proposal (i) _____ in great detail exactly which equipment would be purchased with the grant money and why each piece of equipment was (ii) _____ to make the natural sciences department more (iii) _____.

Blank (i)	Blank (ii)	Blank (iii)
(A) enumerated	(D) contrived	(G) perennial
(B) conjured	(E) forfeited	(H) august
(C) maligned	(F) needed	(I) competitive

Some Text Completions have one blank, and others have two or three. You must use the context of the sentence to replace the blank or blanks with the answer choice that best completes the sentence.

In the first example, the word *wealthy* gives a strong clue to the correct response. The sentence itself sets up a contrast: Although people did wash, only the wealthy washed in one particular way—using heated water. All of the choices are verbs, but only choice D, *afford,* fits the context.

For the second example, you can't simply find a word that fits the first blank; you must find a pair of words that wholly completes the sentence. A valise could be cumbersome or fragile (although probably not "tedious"). However, only choices C and E give you a whole answer. The valise was cumbersome, so Jason had to stop at intervals to relieve his arms and back. None of the other choices work as well.

In the third example, only the word *enumerated* makes contextual sense in blank (i). The proposal would not tell why equipment was contrived or forfeited; it would tell why it was needed. Although *august,* meaning "impressive," could conceivably describe a natural sciences department, the word *competitive* is far more logical as a replacement of blank (iii).

> **FORMAT TIP**
>
> Although they have fewer possible answers, Text Completion questions with two or more blanks can be tricky. The answer choices may offer more than one possibility for each blank. Only by testing both or all three choices as part of the whole can you be sure that your choices are correct. In other words, look at the meaning of the whole sentence, not just at the part or parts you are completing.

▆▆ SOLUTION STRATEGIES: GRE TEXT COMPLETIONS

All of the sentence structure skills that you reviewed in Chapter 6 will come in handy as you prepare to answer Text Completion questions. You will need to recall parts of speech, use context clues, and recognize the meaning of signal words. These questions test your understanding of the way words are put together to create meaning.

Identify Part of Speech

Answer choices for a given Text Completion question will usually be the same part of speech. Nevertheless, you can better understand a cloze sentence if you stop to think: What *kind* of word is missing?

> Although the business partners tried to work out a settlement through mediation, their failure to follow the rules just _____ the conflict.

You need to break down a complex sentence like this into simpler parts. The blank appears in the second clause: *Their failure to follow the rules just _____ the conflict.* The subject of the clause is *failure*. The missing word must be the verb that tells what the failure did to the conflict. A reasonable answer might be *worsened* or *exacerbated*. Thinking about the word you might substitute before you ever read the answer choices can help you recognize which choice is most reasonable.

Use Context Clues

Most words in a sentence are explained by other words in the sentence. The sentence may include examples, explanations, synonyms, antonyms, comparisons, or contrasts that help you determine the meaning of unfamiliar words. Here are some examples.

Example Clue	**Analgesics** such as aspirin are available in most pharmacies.	An *analgesic* is a drug that kills pain.
Explanation Clue	He was considered a **tyro** because he'd never before attempted this particular craft.	A *tyro* is a novice or newcomer to a skill.
Synonym or Definition Clue	Their **perambulation**, or roundabout walk, took place daily at teatime.	A *perambulation* is a roundabout walk.
Antonym Clue	The lecture was **riveting**, not at all dull as we'd been warned.	*Riveting* is the opposite of **dull**.
Comparison Clue	Her speaking voice was as **mellifluous** as the swish of velvet drapes.	A *mellifluous* voice is velvety smooth.
Contrast Clue	Although Hector was **affronted** by the cartoon, Louise found it inoffensive.	To be *affronted* is to be offended.

Use any available clues in a Sentence Completion sentence to determine which of the answer choices best fits the context provided. Here's an example.

> Colleen took a course in _____ that helped her get over her terrible fear of speaking in public.

All the words after *that* provide an explanation that helps to define the missing word. The answer might be *debating, rhetoric,* or *forensics.* It almost certainly will not be *anthropology, genetics,* or *culinary arts.* Can you tell why not?

Try It Yourself

Underline the words in each sentence that give clues to the meaning of the boldfaced word.

1. He tried to **ingratiate** himself with the professor, sucking up to him at all times.

2. Anita loves the taste of cilantro, but her cousin Juana finds it **repugnant**.

3. To our surprise, the critic chose to **disparage** rather than praise the performance.

4. The sparkling lemon drink was as **acrid** as chewing on grapefruit peel.

5. Our class will have a brief **hiatus** in the form of our annual spring break.

Answers and Explanations

1. "Sucking up to" is an explanation of *ingratiate.*

2. "Loves the taste" contrasts with *repugnant,* which means "disgusting."

3. "Rather than praise" is a clue that *disparage* is an antonym for *praise.*

4. "Chewing on grapefruit peel" gives you a sense of the taste described as *acrid.*

5. "Spring break" is an example of one kind of *hiatus,* or time off.

Apply Signal Words

Signal words such as *furthermore, similarly, therefore, despite,* or *because* suggest the meanings of words in a sentence. Words like these are an important part of sentence structure because they define the relationship among the words in the sentence. Here's an example:

> Although he felt strongly about his favorite candidate, Steve found it difficult to _____ why he preferred her to the others.

The signal word *although* indicates that the second clause will be in contrast to the first. Steve feels strongly, but he finds it hard to _____ why he prefers one candidate. He may find it hard to *explain* or *articulate* or *convey* his reasons. Understanding the implied contrast helps you decide what word might complete the sentence.

Try another:

> Jonathan cannot be trusted; moreover, his constant _____ has led many of his longtime friends to drop him.

The signal word *moreover* indicates that the second clause is a continuation of the first. Jonathan cannot be trusted, and this has led his friends to drop him. The missing word must have to do with his untrustworthiness. *Dishonesty, perfidy,* or *duplicity* would be reasonable choices.

For more on signal words, review Chapter 6.

Review Vocabulary

Ultimately, those who perform best on Text Completion questions are those with the greatest vocabularies. Since all the answer choices are likely to be the same parts of speech, your knowledge of their meaning is important to your ability to choose the one that best fits the sentence. Review the vocabulary list and the lists of affixes in Chapter 4. As you practice with the drills that follow, make note of any words whose meanings you do not know.

▨ TEXT COMPLETION DRILL 1

Complete the text by picking the best entry for each blank from the corresponding column of choices. Answers appear at the end of the drill sets.

1. Just as cows look bemused and detached as they chew their cuds, so Luisa had an air of _____ as she chewed gum for hours in class.

A	entertainment
B	studiousness
C	distraction
D	angst
E	resoluteness

2. The actor's performance was so absurdly _____ that Gwen felt a little ashamed to have to resort to tissues in the final scene.

A	proficient
B	unfeasible
C	seditious
D	maudlin
E	accommodating

3. Although his friends insisted that his black garb was simply depressing, Peter felt just the opposite—that it gave him an air of upbeat, _____ maturity.

A	melancholic
B	wearisome
C	salacious
D	aghast
E	urbane

4. The gross negligence of the bank managers seemed so (i) _____ to the general population that the minor (ii) _____ of their underlings inspired little anger at all.

Blank (i)	Blank (ii)
(A) sumptuous	(D) assiduousness
(B) odious	(E) peccadilloes
(C) prosaic	(F) appetites

5. Your (i) _____ do not impress us; furthermore, such false flattery can only serve to (ii) _____ the sincerity of your proposal.

Blank (i)	Blank (ii)
(A) blandishments	(D) vilify
(B) imprecations	(E) dishearten
(C) idylls	(F) counteract

6. Due to the many _____ in his committee presentation, Mark's advisor suggested that he revise his work and practice in front of a mirror before presenting it to the entire department.

(A) facilities
(B) jeremiads
(C) gaffes
(D) obloquies
(E) exploits

7. The wealthy donor was known for his annual acts of (i) _____ throughout the community, but even more (ii) _____ was the fact that he was willing to get his hands dirty and serve the needy through hard physical labor as well as through (iii) _____ and gifts.

Blank (i)	Blank (ii)	Blank (iii)
(A) quality	(D) laudable	(G) effort
(B) legacy	(E) inexpressible	(H) endowments
(C) largesse	(F) disquieting	(I) handiwork

8. The children love to (i) _____ their parents with songs and dances from popular shows; their (ii) _____ hilarity may be heard throughout the neighborhood.

Blank (i)	Blank (ii)
(A) regale	(D) piquant
(B) bestow	(E) raucous
(C) declaim	(F) taciturn

9. Although I consider myself moderately "green," I am not nearly as _____ as my friend Simon, who refuses to eat anything grown more than 50 miles away.

(A) communal
(B) audacious
(C) nebulous
(D) ingratiating
(E) zealous

10. Syria spent a good deal of money attempting to achieve a kind of military (i) _____ with Israel. (ii) _____, its coffers were nearly empty by the mid-1980s, and the Syrian people faced a life of (iii) _____ and hardship.

Blank (i)	Blank (ii)	Blank (iii)
(A) disinterest	(D) In particular	(G) privation
(B) egalitarianism	(E) As a result	(H) redundancy
(C) parity	(F) Without further ado	(I) ennui

TEXT COMPLETION DRILL 2

Complete the text by picking the best entry for each blank from the corresponding column of choices. Answers appear at the end of the drill sets.

1. As the release of the annual report drew near, it was clear that more than a few employees suspected the company was on the verge of bankruptcy; the belief was _____ throughout the organization.

A	omniscient
B	abject
C	pervasive
D	estimable
E	specious

2. Gladys took a _____ approach to problem solving, so when the committee needed ideas on how to create more low-cost public transportation, she suggested they study what worked well in other cities with similar needs.

A	benign
B	pragmatic
C	compliant
D	rarefied
E	dogmatic

3. The jury's verdict was such a surprise that the populace rioted in the streets; nothing less than a reversal of the verdict could _____ them.

A	mollify
B	emulsify
C	denigrate
D	petrify
E	disabuse

4. Political comedy, largely viewed as (i) _____ even in countries in which it is legal and part of the culture, may have an opposite effect on society from the one its creators (ii) _____.

Blank (i)	Blank (ii)
(A) arcane	(D) intend
(B) subversive	(E) demand
(C) pedestrian	(F) redeem

5. The councilman was a highly respected, even (i) _____ member of society, so when he was accused of fraud, people were (ii) _____.

Blank (i)	Blank (ii)
(A) venerated	(D) stunned
(B) obscure	(E) elated
(C) unassuming	(F) gullible

6. Most of the teachers considered the infraction minor; the head of the department, on the other hand, responded with such _____ that it caused the others to rethink their own classroom behavior.

(A) banality
(B) equanimity
(C) reticence
(D) reproof
(E) volition

7. While still a (i) _____ technology, the Internet made dramatic shifts in the way individuals accessed information, communicated with others, and (ii) _____ products on a scale that would have been (iii) _____ a decade earlier.

Blank (i)	Blank (ii)	Blank (iii)
(A) inert	(D) traded	(G) sanctioned
(B) nascent	(E) subsumed	(H) unfathomable
(C) widespread	(F) averted	(I) predictable

8. Some psychologists believe that parents who want to (i) _____ intellectual curiosity in their children should try to answer even the silliest and most (ii) _____ questions the children ask.

Blank (i)	Blank (ii)
(A) betray	(D) implicit
(B) repress	(E) germane
(C) encourage	(F) inane

9. Despite Nathan's _____ toward all things French, he could not help being amused by Rita's reinterpretation of the Molière play.

(A) antipathy
(B) compliance
(C) caginess
(D) confidence
(E) decorum

10. No longer can the town (i) _____ expensive snow removal. (ii) _____ from the date of this new resolution, they will require the townspeople to be responsible for their individual sidewalk (iii) _____.

Blank (i)	Blank (ii)	Blank (iii)
(A) fund	(D) According	(G) decor
(B) tolerate	(E) Starting	(H) clearance
(C) dispute	(F) Inducing	(I) augmentation

Answers and Explanations
Text Completion Drill 1

1. **C.** The clues in the sentence include *bemused* and *detached.* Luisa is said to have the same air as the cows, which means that she, too, is bemused, detached, or distracted.

2. **D.** A performance might be proficient (choice A), but it would not be "absurdly proficient." Gwen might feel some shame at being touched if the performance were *maudlin,* or oversentimental and sappy.

3. **E.** Peter does not believe that his black garb is depressing, so he would not say that it was melancholic (choice A). The only positive choice is *urbane,* meaning "sophisticated."

4. **B, E.** Remember to consider the words in both columns. The gross negligence of the bankers would seem *odious* (hateful), and the *peccadilloes* (minor sins) would fail to inspire anger.

5. **A, F.** The clue *false flattery* should be enough to tell you that the word *blandishments* is a reasonable fit for the first blank. *Counteract* works in the second blank; the sentence means that speaking so falsely works against the proposal's sincerity.

6. **C.** Mark was told to revise and practice his presentation. That indicates that his first go-round was filled with mistakes, or *gaffes.* None of the other words makes sense in context.

7. **C, D, H.** The donor committed acts of *largesse* ("generosity"), which were *laudable* (praiseworthy). Because his physical labor is contrasted with his gifts, the only correct choice for the third blank is (choice H), *endowments.*

8. **A, E.** The fact that the hilarity is "heard throughout the neighborhood" is a solid clue that the noise being made is raucous. The children love to *regale,* or entertain, their parents with this *raucous* diversion.

9. **E.** How would you describe Simon? He is even "greener" than the writer, meaning that he is more *zealous,* or fervent, in his beliefs.

10. **C, E, G.** Think about the logic of the passage. Syria spent its money trying to achieve military *parity,* or equality. That led to a life of hardship, or *privation,* for its people. The privation was a direct result of the overspending.

Text Completion Drill 2

1. **C.** The biggest clue is the phrase *more than a few*. The rumor is *pervasive;* it is widespread.

2. **B.** Following the first comma, the rest of the sentence is an explanation that defines the cloze word. Based on what you are told, you can infer that Gladys has a *pragmatic,* or practical, approach to problem solving.

3. **A.** If the populace is rioting, it needs to be calmed, which is what a reversal of the verdict might do. The best choice is *mollify,* which means "calm down."

4. **B, D.** Even where it's legal, political comedy might be viewed as *subversive,* or rebellious. Its effect may be other than the one its creators *intend.*

5. **A, D.** He was not just respected, he was *venerated* (choice A). People would not be *elated* if such a person were accused of fraud, so the answer to the second blank must be choice D, *stunned.*

6. **D.** If you don't immediately know the answer, use the process of elimination to get rid of the answers that just don't fit. Most people thought the infraction was minor. The head of the department is contrasted with those people, so he must have thought the infraction was major and reacted in kind. The answer, *reproof,* means "scolding."

7. **B, D, H.** The sentence is set in the past, at a time when the Internet was newborn, or *nascent* (choice B). The dramatic shifts allowed people to trade products in a way that would have been *unfathomable,* or unthinkable, a decade earlier. None of the other choices makes sense in context.

8. **C, F.** Parents may want to *encourage* curiosity in their children. The word *silliest* calls for a synonym in the second blank, and the only synonym is *inane.*

9. **A.** The word *despite* sets up a contrast between the opening phrase and the independent clause in the sentence. Nathan is amused by the play even though he doesn't find French things amusing—he has an *antipathy,* or dislike, for them.

10. **A, E, H**. Although *tolerate* is possible, *fund* makes much more sense in context. The town will require people to clear their own sidewalks, not decorate or add to them, and that change will start with the date of the new resolution.

CHAPTER 9

GRE READING COMPREHENSION QUESTIONS

CHAPTER GOALS

• Study examples of Reading Comprehension passages and questions.

• Learn specific strategies for answering Reading Comprehension questions.

• Practice answering sample GRE Reading Comprehension questions.

As you learned in Chapter 5, Reading Comprehension on the GRE is tested using up to a dozen nonfiction passages of a paragraph or more, each of which is followed by questions. The object is to see how well you understand and analyze short pieces of informational writing of the sort that you might regularly read at the college and graduate level.

Reading these passages, however, is not like reading material for a class. You need to retain the information found in each one for a very short period of time—just long enough to answer the questions.

ITEM FORMAT: GRE READING COMPREHENSION

The format of some GRE Reading Comprehension questions is identical to formats you have seen on tests throughout your school career. You are given a brief passage. The question consists of a question stem and five answer choices.

> The Arecibo Observatory, near the north shore of Puerto Rico, is a key component of Cornell University's National Astronomy and Ionosphere Center (NAIC). In a joint venture with the National Science Foundation, the observatory exists to provide observation time and support for scientists worldwide. A panel of judges determines the "most promising" research proposals among the hun-

dreds that are presented to the observatory each year. Those scientists are invited to Puerto Rico for viewing time on Arecibo's giant telescope.

The Arecibo telescope does not resemble what most of us think of when we hear the word *telescope*. Its reflective surface covers a remarkable 20 acres. Dangling above it are towers and cables, sub-reflectors and antennas, all of which can be positioned using 26 motors to transmit radio waves and receive echoes with astonishing precision.

It can be inferred from the final paragraph that most telescopes

(A) do not have reflective surfaces

(B) contain radio antennas

(C) are not as large as Arecibo's

(D) cannot be repositioned

(E) are made in Puerto Rico

To answer this particular question, you must look specifically at the last paragraph. Those sentences refer to the scope of the telescope and to its parts and function. A GRE Reading Comprehension question will never go beyond what is stated or implied by the passage. There is nothing in those sentences to suggest that choice A, B, D, or E is true. On the other hand, the word *remarkable* indicates that Arecibo's massive size makes it different from other telescopes, so the best answer is choice C.

Two other formats exist on the new GRE. In the first, you must choose among three responses and select all that apply. Your answer may be one, two, or all three responses.

Consider each of the choices separately and select all that apply.

The author of the passage suggests which of the following about the scientists who use Arecibo's telescope?

(A) They may use the telescope by invitation only.

(B) They must be affiliated with Cornell University.

(C) They first submit proposals to a panel of judges.

Information to answer this question appears in the first paragraph. Although Arecibo itself is affiliated with Cornell, there is no indication that such an affiliation is a prerequisite for using the telescope. That eliminates choice B as a response. However, both choice A and choice C are supported by the last two sentences of the paragraph: "A panel of judges determines the 'most promising' research proposals among the hundreds that are presented to the observatory each year. Those scientists are invited to Puerto Rico for viewing time on Arecibo's giant telescope." You would need to select both choice A and choice C to receive credit for this response.

The last Reading Comprehension format is one that you will see only occasionally. You are asked to select a sentence that fits a particular description or request. On the computerized test, you will click anywhere in the sentence to highlight it. For our purposes here, you may underline it.

Underline the sentence that suggests that scientists from Asia or Africa may spend time working at Arecibo.

To answer this question, you must scan the article to locate a single sentence that fits the parameters requested. Since Asia and Africa are never mentioned, you must look more closely for the sentence that hints at Arecibo's use by scientists from other lands. The only sentence that does this is: "In a joint venture with the National Science Foundation, the observatory exists to provide observation time and support for scientists worldwide." That is the sentence you would highlight (or underline) in the passage.

SOLUTION STRATEGIES: GRE READING COMPREHENSION

The reading strategies in Chapter 5 will help you *prepare* for the test. The strategies here will help you as you *take* the test.

Preview the Passage

If the passage is divided into paragraphs, read the first paragraph to get a sense of what the passage is about. Then skim the rest of the passage. This means that you should not slow down to figure out the meaning of any unfamiliar words, and you should not search for more than the general idea of each paragraph. Remember, time is a factor here. You have 30 minutes to answer 20 Verbal Reasoning questions. You cannot spend 5 of those minutes dissecting and analyzing a short reading passage.

Skim the Question Stems

Typically, two or more questions will follow the passage. After skimming the passage quickly, glance over the question stems—not the answer choices. This will give you a good sense of what to look for as you read the passage more carefully. For example, if a question stem asks about a particular topic that you remember from your skimming, you can easily relocate that topic in the passage and answer the question by reading that part of the passage more closely.

As you skim the question stems, you may find that you're able to predict an answer. This will help you as you select among given answer choices.

Reread for Specifics

Armed with your understanding of what the questions will ask, return to the passage and reread specifically to find the information asked for in each question. Then test your prediction against the answer choices.

Try It Yourself

Read the following question stem. For each of the two passages that follow it, circle the section that answers the question. Possible answers are given after the exercise.

The author's attitude toward Congress might best be described as . . .

Passage 1

> As Congress meets to come to terms with the economic crisis, it's too much to expect a nonpartisan meeting of the minds, given the infighting of the past eight years. Senators and representatives will meet in committee and then present a final recommendation to both houses before the self-imposed deadline.

Passage 2

> Congressman Atwood arrived in Washington with no legislative experience, a small but dedicated staff, and one of the smallest offices of any representative. Following his recent re-election, he remains in the tiny office, but he is an experienced legislator. The first term in Congress is always a trial by fire, but Congress protects and trains its newcomers like a fierce mother tiger.

Answers and Explanations

In the first paragraph, the section that expresses the author's attitude is "it's too much to expect a nonpartisan meeting of the minds, given the infighting of the past eight years." The author's attitude might be described as *resigned* or *fed up*. In the second paragraph, the section that expresses the author's attitude is "Congress protects and trains its newcomers like a fierce mother tiger." The author's attitude might be described as *impressed* or *satisfied*.

Use the Process of Elimination

Eliminate any choices that are obviously incorrect. Eliminate any choices that go beyond what is stated or implied by the passage. Before zeroing in on one choice, read the choices carefully to be sure that the wording matches what you are asked in the question stem.

Understand the Word *Except*

An occasional question may include the word *except,* as in this example:

All of these are mentioned in the passage as Edison inventions EXCEPT

- (A) the disc phonograph
- (B) the kinetoscope
- (C) the parallel circuit
- (D) the film projector
- (E) the metal detector

You can express the question stem in a different way: "Which of these is NOT mentioned in the passage as an Edison invention?" That may help you to zero in on the one invention that is not Edison's (in this case, E, the metal detector, which was invented by Alexander Graham Bell).

Do not fall into the trap of thinking "Edison invention" and then choosing the first Edison invention you see listed. Questions like this are asking for the *exception* on the list.

Use a Five-Step Process with "Select All" Questions

As you have seen, the GRE may present you with a question like this one:

Consider each of the choices separately and select all that apply.

According to the passage, Dickens and Austen are similar in which of the following ways?

- (A) Both are concerned with class differences.
- (B) Both rely on humorous secondary characters.
- (C) Both satirize traditional values.

The process to use as you answer such a question has five steps.

1. Read and understand the question stem. In this case, you are being asked to find the way or ways in which Dickens and Austen are similar. You are given three possible ways: choices A, B, and C.
2. Read choice A and ask yourself whether it is true according to the passage. (Remember, if it is not specifically mentioned in the passage, it cannot be considered true; the question stem says "According to the passage.") Is it true? Yes or no?
3. Read choice B and decide whether it is true according to the passage.
4. Read choice C and decide whether it is true according to the passage.
5. Use each of your "yes" and "no" determinations to select the correct answer choice or choices. (In this particular case, you have no passage to read, but the answer is most likely choices A, B, and C, which you may think of as "all of the above.")

FORMAT TIP

Do not be alarmed if you find only one correct solution for a "select all" question. Any such question may have one, two, or three solutions.

READING COMPREHENSION DRILL 1

Read the passage and answer the questions. Answers appear at the end of the drill sets.

Questions 1–3 are based on the following passage.

Purple loosestrife, with its attractive spiky stems and flowers, does not just propagate and cross-pollinate wildly; it also adapts easily to changes in environment. As it starts up in a new area, it quickly outcompetes native grasses, sedges, and other flowering plants, forming dense stands of purple loosestrife where once heterogeneous wetland meadows existed. This not only eradicates the native plants, but also it removes food sources for migratory birds and other animals.

In recent years, purple loosestrife has had a devastating impact on native cattails and wild rice. It has invaded and destroyed spawning areas for fish. In rural areas, it is beginning to move away from wetlands and adapt to drier areas, encroaching on agricultural lands. In urban areas, it is blocking pipes and drainage canals. It has moved steadily westward and is now found in all states but Florida.

Attempts to control purple loosestrife have been only partially successful. It has proved resistant to many herbicides, and it is impervious to burning, as its rootstock lies beneath the surface and can reproduce from there. It can be mowed down and plowed under, and then replaced with a less invasive plant. This is very labor intensive in marshy areas that are substantially overgrown, but it may be the only way of eliminating the pest.

1. According to the passage, all of these are true EXCEPT:

   (A) Purple loosestrife propagates through an underground system.

   (B) Purple loosestrife has even affected the survival of fish.

   (C) Purple loosestrife is best eradicated through controlled burning.

   (D) Purple loosestrife is sometimes found in urban areas.

   (E) Purple loosestrife is found in the wetlands of most states.

For questions 2 and 3, consider each of the choices separately and select all that apply.

2. Which fact or facts about purple loosestrife add to its power of endurance?

   A It has a great ability to cross-pollinate.

   B It easily adapts to environmental change.

   C It has spiky stems and flowers.

3. According to the passage, where would purple loosestrife easily thrive?

   A in the subtropical swamps of central Florida

   B in the wetland meadows of eastern Michigan

   C along the inland waterways of North Carolina

READING COMPREHENSION DRILL 2

Read the passage and answer the questions. Answers appear at the end of the drill sets.

Questions 1–3 are based on the following passage.

The Cockneys developed their own vernacular over a hundred years or so, and during the early part of the nineteenth century, rhyming slang became an integral part of this argot. It was associated in many Londoners' minds with the underworld, since it could easily be used as a sort of code. For their own self-preservation, Scotland Yard began to publish translations of the slang in police manuals, and thus the strange colloquialisms began to cross out of the East End and into the general population.

The rules behind the rhyming slang are as simple as the result is clever and difficult to comprehend. A speaker puts together words, the last of which rhymes with the word he or she means to denote. For example, *loaf of bread* might mean "head." The difficulty comes as the slang becomes widespread and the original rhyme is discarded as superfluous, so that *loaf* means "head" in a sentence such as "He gave his loaf a thump."

1. The author of the passage would probably agree that rhyming slang is

   (A) overrated

   (B) ingenious

   (C) superfluous

   (D) undemanding

   (E) immature

2. Underline the sentence that shows that, to the police, rhyming slang was a troublesome barrier.

3. According to the rules for forming Cockney rhyming slang in paragraph 2, which word might be rhyming slang for *house*?

   (A) *Cat,* from "cat and mouse"

   (B) *Rat,* from "dirty rat"

   (C) *Home,* from "house and home"

   (D) *Louse,* from "dirty louse"

   (E) *Boat,* from "houseboat"

Answers and Explanations
Reading Comprehension Drill 1

1. **C.** Skim to locate mention of four out of five assertions. The underground system (choice A) appears in paragraph 3. Purple loosestrife's effect on fish appears in paragraph 2, as does its appearance in urban areas and in most states. Paragraph 3 says that it is "impervious to burning," making choice C the best answer.

2. **A, B.** All three details are facts about purple loosestrife, but only its ability to cross-pollinate (choice A) and its easy adaptability (choice B) are facts that "add to its power of endurance."

3. **B, C.** You must extrapolate the answer based on what you have learned about purple loosestrife from the passage. Because it thrives in wetlands and along rivers, either choice B or choice C is likely. Although choice A might in theory be possible, the author does point out, "It has moved steadily westward and is now found in all states but Florida."

Reading Comprehension Drill 2

1. **B.** The author talks about the convoluted process of creating rhyming slang in a tone that appears to appreciate its difficulty. The best answer is choice B.

2. **"For their own self-preservation, Scotland Yard began to publish translations of the slang in police manuals, and thus the strange colloquialisms began to cross out of the East End and into the general population."** The discussion of Scotland Yard tells of police publishing translations of rhyming slang in their manuals. The implication is that rhyming slang was causing them problems, and they needed to understand it better to perform their jobs.

3. **A.** Cockney rhyming slang begins with a rhyming phrase, but often, as the author states, "the original rhyme is discarded as superfluous." In the passage, the example given is *loaf of bread* for "head" becoming simply *loaf.* The only example from the answer choices that follows this pattern is choice A, with *cat and mouse* dropping off *and mouse* to leave simply *cat.*

CHAPTER 10

GRE ANALYTICAL WRITING

CHAPTER GOALS

- Learn about special features of GRE Analytical Writing.

- Recognize the two tasks: the Issue Task and the Argument Task.

- Learn specific strategies for planning an essay.

- Practice writing GRE Issue Task and Argument Task essays.

- Study sample essays and compare them to your own responses.

Analytical Writing is always the first part of the GRE that you will tackle. In this part of the test, you will complete two tasks, each of which involves writing an essay. The tasks and essay topics are independent of each other. For each task, you will have 30 minutes. This time includes any prewriting and editing you wish to do.

Analytical Writing is scored separately from the rest of the Verbal Reasoning part of the GRE. Some graduate programs do not use the Analytical Writing score. Such programs may have their own writing assignment as part of the application process. Nevertheless, the Analytical Writing score will be reported along with your other GRE scores, so it's worth preparing for the essays whether or not your chosen program relies upon them to evaluate you as an applicant.

You will type your essays using a special word processing program. It is not as sophisticated as the programs you may be used to. It will allow you to cut, copy, and paste. If you're the kind of writer who prefers to dive in and write the body of an essay before crafting an introduction and conclusion, you can do that quite nicely on the GRE. However, you won't be able to insert charts, check the thesaurus, or use fancy formatting.

ITEM FORMAT: GRE ISSUE TASK

The point of the Issue Task is to support a position on a given issue. There are no right or wrong answers. It does not matter at all what stance you choose to take; you earn no extra points for agreeing or disagreeing with the prompt. Because the programs you're applying for will get a copy of your essays, it may be best not to take a stance that is radically controversial, but other than that, you won't hurt your score or application by expressing an opinion that isn't really your own.

Issue prompts and directions look something like this:

Issue Topic

> "The most important learning we do takes place outside of the classroom and away from teachers and peers."
>
> Discuss the extent to which you agree or disagree with the claim made above. Use relevant reasons and examples to support your point of view.

You are asked to present your viewpoint and to use reasons and examples in support of the perspective you choose. The readers who assess your writing will look for your ability to present that viewpoint clearly and to support it solidly and logically.

There is no one correct answer to the prompt. Readers will not be looking for a classic "five-paragraph essay," nor do they care whether you use a particular organization or a set number of reasons or examples. They will grade you on your clarity, the strength of your argument, and your ability to use Standard English correctly.

SOLUTION STRATEGIES: GRE ISSUE TASK

Since you do not know precisely what topics you will be given on your GRE, it's difficult to prepare for this part of the test. You can hone your thinking and writing skills, however, and the strategies that follow will help you focus on the task.

Scan the Prompts

The GRE website (www.ets.org/gre) provides the exact prompts from which test writers will choose. Do yourself a favor and look these over. A pool of writing topics appears in the "Prepare for the Test" section under the GRE General Test. You won't be able to memorize them all (and the wording may be changed slightly when they appear on the test), but scanning the list and making sure you understand each prompt is a good way to get started.

Try Some Timed Writing

Writing with the clock ticking can be daunting. It's worth testing yourself with the sort of 30-minute deadline you'll have for the Issue Task. Pick one or two of the writing topics that appear on the GRE website and give them a try. Set a kitchen timer. Consider using this time breakdown:

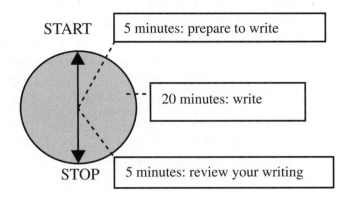

START — 5 minutes: prepare to write

20 minutes: write

STOP — 5 minutes: review your writing

Spending a little time organizing your thoughts and a little time cleaning up your grammar and mechanics will pay off in your score. Remember, you are judged on your organization and on your proper use of Standard English. The more you write and time yourself, the better you will be at judging how quickly to write when you take the actual test.

Practice Picking a Position

Once you've read over the topic, you must pick a position to respond to the claim. Suppose you start with this topic.

> "The most important learning we do takes place outside of the classroom and away from teachers and peers."

There are a variety of positions you could take in response to this prompt.

- Yes, the most important learning we do takes place outside of the classroom and away from teachers and peers.
- No, the most important learning we do actually does take place in the classroom with teachers and peers.
- The most important learning we do takes place in a variety of environments—both in the classroom and outside.
- The most important learning we do takes place outside of the classroom, but we need the companionship of teachers and peers to allow us to test our ideas.

You can see that this is not necessarily a black-and-white argument; it may contain shades of gray. That's fine. What's important is that you consider more than one point of view on the issue before you begin to write. You will need to incorporate the pros and the cons as you construct your argument.

Consider Pros and Cons

A sensible way to construct a response to the Issue Task is to begin by showing the pros of the position you choose. In that opening paragraph, it is perfectly acceptable to include one or two negatives involving your position—as long as your pros are stronger and more meaningful. Remember, you will spend five minutes organizing your thoughts before you write. You might outline such a paragraph this way:

```
I.   Important learning doesn't need to take place in a
     classroom
     A.   Best thinking takes place alone--meditation, etc.
     B.   Many key American innovations, inventions have been
          individual (give examples).
     C.   Sometimes it's useful to have someone to bounce ideas
          off of--but that's best done once we've absorbed the
          issues and done our own careful thinking.
```

You can see that as you're outlining the opening paragraph, you're thinking about examples that support your position.

A second paragraph can concern itself with the counterargument—the side opposing your position. Your goal here is to show that although the opposite side is not entirely wrong, it is not as reasonable as the position you've chosen. You understand the other side; you just consider it misguided.

```
II.  Counterargument: important learning does take place in
     the classroom.
     A.   People think we need experts or elders to show us the
          way (but many of us learn best by reading those ex-
          perts rather than by talking about them).
     B.   Modern America emphasizes teamwork (but America was
          built on individualism).
```

Notice that as you list items that support the other side, you may be considering ways to tear them down. You can lay out the other side's position and then counter it with a clause that begins with *but, however,* or *on the other hand.*

Now you have two full paragraphs, one building your position, and the other explaining but countering the opposing position. You can wrap up your essay with a concluding paragraph that brings your position home to the reader.

```
III. Our best learning happens when we're on our own
     A.  Need for individual contemplation.
     B.  "Quiet mind" allows for enlightenment.
     C.  Only when we know ourselves can we begin to share
         knowledge with others.
```

Here you see that your essay ends with a return to the opposing position. You haven't completely rejected the idea of learning with others, but your position is that self-knowledge is a prerequisite to that kind of learning.

Thinking in terms of pros and cons will help you organize the Issue Task. Depending on your ideas and speed, you may wish to write four or five paragraphs instead of three, but three will certainly allow you to do what needs to be done. You will not be graded on the length of your essay.

SCORING THE GRE ISSUE TASK

Readers score your GRE essays using a holistic rubric that ranges from 0 to 6. Here is what those scores mean for the Issue Task.

Score	Focus	Organization	Conventions
0	Does not address the chosen prompt. Off topic.	Incomprehensible. May merely copy the prompt without development.	Illegible. Nonverbal. Serious errors make the paper unreadable. May be in a foreign language.
1	Mostly irrelevant to the chosen prompt.	Little or no development of ideas. No evidence of analysis or organization.	Pervasive errors in grammar, mechanics, and spelling.
2	Unclear connection to the chosen prompt.	Unfocused and disorganized.	Frequent errors in sentence structure, mechanics, and spelling.
3	Limited connection to the chosen prompt.	Rough organization with weak examples or reasons.	Occasional major errors and frequent minor errors in conventions of written English.
4	Competent connection to the chosen prompt.	Relevant examples or reasons develop a logical position.	Occasional minor errors in conventions of written English.
5	Clear, focused connection to the chosen prompt.	Thoughtful, appropriate examples or reasons develop a consistent, coherent position. Connectors are ably used to mark transitions.	Very few errors. Sentence structure is varied, and vocabulary is advanced.
6	Insightful, clever connection to the chosen prompt.	Compelling, convincing examples or reasons develop a consistent, coherent position. The argument flows effortlessly and persuasively.	Very few errors. Sentence structure is varied, and vocabulary is precise, well chosen, and effective.

Try It Yourself

Use the following prompt to write your own timed essay.

Issue Topic

> "Rebellion is a necessary part of growing up. If young people fail to rebel, they fail to develop their own personalities."
>
> Discuss the extent to which you agree or disagree with the claim made below. Use relevant reasons and examples to support your point of view.

Turn off the grammar- and spell-checker on your word processor. Take 5 minutes to plan and outline your response. Leave 5 minutes at the end to check and revise your essay. Set your timer for 30 minutes.

When you finish, compare your essay to the following scored essays.

Issue Task Essay: Score of 6

This essay is fluent and coherent. It addresses the prompt in an insightful way by showing the results of certain types of rebellions throughout history and by indicating that rebellion is not the negative force a counterargument might find it to be.

Parents and teachers alike are frequently frustrated by the seemingly random rebellions of their young charges, but they should rest assured that such minor insurgencies are a critical part of the growing-up process. If they can learn to see adolescent rebellion for what it truly is-- a testing of boundaries, a trying-on of personalities, a necessary loosening of the bonds between adult and child-- adults will take it in stride instead of fighting it tooth and nail, and both adults and adolescents will have an easier time during this significant period in their lives.

Adolescent rebellion may seem particularly offensive to parents who believe they have given their children every opportunity. We all know parents who feel threatened if their children seem to know more about a topic than they do. There is even a culture of home-schoolers who, one suspects, home-school precisely so that their children don't outgrow them in any way. This is understandable, but it is also sad. If children never surpass their parents in any way, doesn't that portend a stagnant culture?

If young people fail to rebel, to question authority and resist conformity, they might as well be clones of their parents. It is through this questioning and resistance that they move forward toward the development of their own unique personalities. Many will find through their rebellion that--surprise!--father really does know best. Others will discover a new way to be that eschews a parent's racism or classism in favor of an open mind and heart. Still others may entirely overthrow the culture that raised them and head off in a different direction. That may be a painful break, but it is not necessarily wrong.

In America, especially, we should celebrate rebellion, for ours is a nation of rebels. The adolescent colonies rose up against the adult Europeans, and the world was changed, I believe, for the better. Our grandparents' generation rebelled against the immigrant culture that spoke other languages at home, and the result was the best-educated generation the world had ever seen. Our parents' generation rebelled against a political stodginess that enmeshed us in foreign wars. When our own children rebel--and it's fascinating to think how that might manifest itself--I hope we can accept it as a natural part of the continuum of life.

Issue Task Essay: Score of 4

This essay is competent and logical. It addresses the prompt with simple but relevant examples. There are lapses in conventional English ("straight-laced," "everyone would dress like their parents," "their parents business"), but they do not interfere with a reader's understanding.

Rebellion is a necessary part of growing up because it helps someone determine what they are going to be. The child of a professor might want to farm the land. The child of a barber might want to dance in the City Ballet. Without breaking away from the family to some degree, such changes would not be possible.

In my experience, it is not only the children of strict or straight-laced parents who tend to rebel. The daughter of a wild New York City musician I know decided to be a high school cheerleader. The son of a carpenter in a commune now sells insurance and is a rector in his church. Teenage rebellion is more about finding one's way than about tearing down the status quo.

Teenage rebellion can cause difficulties in the household. It can mean daily drama and out-and-out battles between parents and children. It is never a pleasant rite of passage. Still, we would be worse off without it.

Picture a world without teenage rebellion. Everyone would dress like their parents and go into their parents business without question. That would-be ballerina would never get the chance to stretch her wings and fly. The would-be farmer wouldn't develop new ways of raising crops. The world would miss out on what they might have to offer.

We all need to break away to find our true selves. The "helicopter parents" of today aren't doing their children any favors. Their assumption seems to be that their children cannot cope without their help, but the reality is that their children cannot grow up unless they break away, rebel, and find their own pathway through life.

Issue Task Essay: Score of 2

This essay is vague and disorganized. It does pick a position and address the prompt, but the examples given are unclear, and the flow of ideas seems slapdash rather than thoughtful. There is no attempt to address potential counterarguments, and the conclusion is dubious. Many lapses in conventional English may interfere with a reader's understanding.

Rebellion is a necessary part of growing up to develop your own personality. As a child you might not have a real personality, it might instead be what your parents want from you, or your peers with peer pressure. To develop your own personality you most likely need to have a rebellion of sorts.

For example, you might be a teenager who decides not to go to college, unlike your parents dreams. That is a kind of rebellion that can seem pretty negative out of which some posative could come. Or if you go to college, you might decide to major in something that your parents don't agree with, for example art or another subject area.

That can lead to a lot of fights between the family but it is still something out of which some posative can come. For example, you might be a great artist. Your rebellion (I want to major in art) leads you to your new personality (great artist). As well, you don't need to be disrespectful when you rebel, it's possible to rebel

```
without being mean or offendsive but instead calm and
respectful of other peoples opinions and ideas.
    So rebellion is important if you want to do something
great. Without rebelling from your parents ideas of
who you should be, you may not be able to develop the
personality you desire.
```

ITEM FORMAT: GRE ARGUMENT TASK

Unlike the Issue Task, which requires you to choose sides on an issue and support your decision, the Argument Task requires you to critique an existing argument. Instead of presenting your own reasons and examples, you must analyze given evidence to see whether it supports a given conclusion.

The Argument prompt and directions look like this:

Argument Topic

The following letter was sent to voters in a local school district.

"As you know, there is talk of consolidating our schools by closing Twin Lakes Elementary and moving those children to the larger school at Beaver Creek. This goes against what we know about the value of neighborhood schools. Studies show that small schools, defined as schools of 300 to 500 students, provide more in the way of teacher-student contact, which in turn improves student achievement. Twin Lakes, with just 95 students, offers our students even more. Studies also indicate that class size has a positive effect on student achievement at the primary grades. Twin Lakes averages only 16 students per grade level. Closing Twin Lakes may save a bit of money, but it will also mean certain failure for many of our students who are doing well right now."

Critique the reasoning used in this argument by examining assumptions, assessing evidence, and/or suggesting ways to make the argument stronger or easier to evaluate.

The argument is laid out for you; you must determine which aspects of it are logical and reasonable and which are not. Any GRE Argument Task will have substantial flaws that you are meant to discover.

Once again, your readers will grade you on your clarity, the strength of your analysis, and your ability to use Standard English correctly. You will also be graded on your ability to evaluate the logical credibility of an argument.

SOLUTION STRATEGIES: GRE ARGUMENT TASK

Although this sort of writing and thinking is absolutely essential to your work in graduate school, you may not be used to dissecting arguments in this way. These strategies will help you understand what you are supposed to do.

Scan the Prompts

Once again, scan the pool of writing topics in the "Prepare for the Text" section under the GRE General Test on the GRE website. Your test Argument Task will be selected from among those listed on the site. Knowing what to expect gives you a leg up on the competition. You can also use the prompts to practice this form of writing, which may be unfamiliar to you.

Try Some Timed Writing

Again, you'll have 30 minutes for the Argument Task. Consider keeping the same amount of prewriting and postwriting time as you plan your essay.

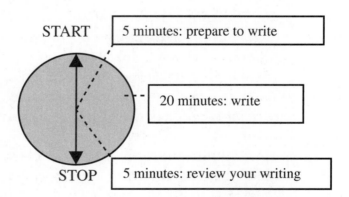

START   5 minutes: prepare to write

20 minutes: write

STOP   5 minutes: review your writing

That prewriting 5-minute interval can mean the difference between a well-planned essay and a stream-of-consciousness mess. The postwriting interval allows you to catch any errors in structure, spelling, or punctuation. Remember, you won't have spell-checking or grammar-checking capability as you take the test.

Know the Basics of Logic

To determine whether the logic in an Argument Task passage is sound, it helps to take a crash course in the basics of logic. A classic logical argument can be stated in *if . . . then* form:

> IF a pig is a mammal, and
> IF a mammal is warm-blooded,
> THEN a pig is warm-blooded.

The "IF" statements are *evidence,* and the "THEN" statement is the conclusion. An argument may be considered *valid* if it follows this structure. However, if either or both of the pieces of evidence are false, the conclusion is likely to be false as well, as in this example:

> IF a fish is a mammal, and
> IF a mammal is warm-blooded,
> THEN a fish is warm-blooded.

A fish is not a mammal, so the conclusion is not true. The argument, therefore, is not *sound.*

There are many ways to construct an unsound argument, or *fallacy.* To succeed on the GRE Argument Task, you must look for the fallacies and explain how they unbalance the argument. Here are some fallacies you may encounter as you read the Argument Task passage.

Ad Hominem *Arguments*—These are arguments directed against the person making the argument rather than against the soundness of the argument itself. For example:

> Since all of them are over 65, and many have disabilities, the residents of the home cannot be expected to have an opinion on the proposed neighborhood skateboard park.

The assumption that because they are elderly or disabled the residents have no opinion is clearly a fallacy. They may object to the potential noise or be eager to see young people involved in a pastime that keeps them off the street. There's no way of telling; the fallacy stops all such reasoning in its tracks.

Appeal to Authority—You may see this type of argument in an advertising campaign. Someone is held up as an authority even when his or her expertise in the area is questionable, as in this example:

> Phil Carter, who has played an emergency room doctor for 20 years on the nation's most popular soap opera, testified before Congress today on the need for more nursing schools.

Mr. Carter may be well-intentioned, but what possible value does his testimony have?

Appeal to Belief/Appeal to Majority—Just because a lot of people believe it does not make it so, as in this example:

> The power of prayer is clearly legitimate; nearly 8 out of 10 Americans believe that prayer cures disease.

Belief by itself cannot legitimize an argument.

Appeal to Emotion—Politicians use this one every day. Just because something makes you feel good doesn't mean it's valid, true, or sound:

> Who wouldn't want to help these sad, orphaned children? Giving just a few dollars a month will change their lives and yours forever.

Maybe it will change their lives, but the evidence shown is not enough to prove that. Maybe it will change your life; maybe it will just lighten your wallet.

Begging the Question—In this sort of fallacy, the conclusion is assumed to be true, and that assumption appears in the evidence, as here:

> If pushing mortgages on people who can't afford them were unethical, it would be against the law. Since it isn't illegal, it must be ethical.

Not really. There's nothing that says that *unethical* and *illegal* are equivalent—except the fallacy itself.

Biased Sample—If you use statistics that are based on a sample with built-in bias, your conclusion is naturally suspect. For example:

> A study recently found that 50 percent of Americans prefer to vacation near the ocean. The survey was conducted by telephone in North Carolina, California, and Maine.

Since all three states surveyed border the ocean, the study suffers from a built-in bias. You might be able to conclude that 50 percent of Americans in ocean-bordering states prefer to vacation near the ocean, but unless you poll people farther inland, you cannot draw the conclusion given.

Confusing Causation—Just because two events happen at the same time or one after the other does not mean that one has caused the other. Consider this example:

> People who are stressed due to troubled relationships or work environments often experience depression. Stress is therefore a cause of depression.

Maybe it is, and maybe it isn't. Trouble at home and work might easily cause both stress and depression, but that doesn't mean that stress itself causes depression.

Hasty Generalization—If you draw a conclusion from too small a sample, your conclusion cannot be considered sound. For example:

> Joe drives to the store and is cut off in the parking lot by an elderly woman in a BMW. He immediately calls his wife to rail about the fact that (1) old people can't drive and (2) rich people don't care about anything but themselves.

We make these sorts of generalizations all day long, but that doesn't mean they're reasonable.

Red Herring—This is the name for an irrelevant fact stuck in the middle of an argument to draw attention away from the central issue. As you analyze an argument, do not be distracted by red herrings like this one:

> We will doubtless need to cut a handful of staff positions to handle the current budget crunch, but remember, thousands stood in breadlines during the Great Depression.

Comparing your budget woes favorably to the Great Depression may temporarily distract people from the fact that their jobs are in jeopardy, but it's really just a red herring.

Reductio ad Absurdum—You may use this one to show the errors in an existing argument. Basically, you draw parallels between a silly argument and a truly absurd one to show the illogic in the silly one, as here:

> My stomach hasn't hurt since last week, when I started taking Vitamin C. Vitamin C must have a curative effect on sour stomach.

> I haven't had a headache since last week, when I started conditioning my hair with hot oil. Hot oil must have a curative effect on headaches.

The cause-and-effect relationship is tenuous in the first example, and downright ridiculous in the second.

Slippery Slope—The slippery slope occurs when the conclusion contains unsupported predictions of inevitability. One event leads (or might lead) to another, which leads (or might lead) to a third, and so on, until the conclusion is so far removed from the original evidence that it is suspect, as in this example:

> It's ridiculous that my son's school prevents access to social networking sites. It doesn't allow outside e-mailing, either. It won't be long before America emulates a third-world dictatorship and just bans the Internet entirely.

Whether or not banning social networking sites is "ridiculous," the speaker's conclusion doesn't follow from the evidence and therefore doesn't present a sound argument.

Straw Man—A straw man fallacy is based on a misrepresentation of someone's argument in an effort to present a counterargument, as here:

> The mayor says she intends to place the new parking garage next to Floral Park. Obviously, open space is not a priority of this administration.

You cannot assume a bias against open space based on this single example. The mayor's placement of the garage does not mean that she rejects open space.

Organize Your Attack

No matter what prompt you are given, your job will be to deconstruct it and to pick out its flaws. You may do this in several ways, two of which are shown here. Each Roman numeral represents a paragraph.

```
   I. Review the prompt; give an overview of its flaws.

  II. First problem with the argument.

 III. Second problem with the argument.

  IV. Third problem with the argument.

   V. Conclusion: Why the argument isn't sound; some
      possibilities for improvement.
```

This organization yields a basic five-paragraph essay with an introduction and conclusion. Each of the paragraphs in the body dissects one specific flaw you have discovered in the argument. If you find more than three, you might add paragraphs. If you find two, you might end up with a four-paragraph essay.

Here is another means of organizing your essay.

```
   I. Review the prompt, give an overview of its flaws.

  II. Analysis of assumptions made by the author.

 III. Analysis of evidence provided by the author.

  IV. Analysis of conclusion drawn by the author.

   V. Conclusion: Why the argument isn't sound; some
      possibilities for improvement.
```

This organization breaks down the argument into assumptions, evidence, and conclusions made by the author of the prompt. By analyzing all three, you are likely to touch on most of the flaws in the argument.

Remember, you may choose any organization that works for you. The goal is to find a way to address the task that is clear and logical.

SCORING THE GRE ARGUMENT TASK

Remember that readers score your GRE essays using a holistic rubric that ranges from 0 to 6. Here is what those scores mean for the Argument Task.

Score	Focus	Organization	Conventions
0	Does not address the prompt. Off topic.	Incomprehensible. May merely copy the prompt without development.	Illegible. Nonverbal. Serious errors make the paper unreadable. May be in a foreign language.
1	Little or no analysis of the argument. May indicate misunderstanding of the prompt.	Little or no development of ideas. No evidence of analysis or organization.	Pervasive errors in grammar, mechanics, and spelling.
2	Little analysis; may instead present opinions and unrelated thoughts.	Disorganized and illogical.	Frequent errors in sentence structure, mechanics, and spelling.
3	Some analysis of the prompt, but some major flaws may be omitted.	Rough organization with irrelevant support or unclear transitions.	Occasional major errors and frequent minor errors in conventions of written English.
4	Important flaws in the argument are touched upon.	Ideas are sound but may not flow logically or clearly.	Occasional minor errors in conventions of written English.
5	Perceptive analysis of the major flaws in the argument.	Logical examples and support develop a consistent, coherent critique. Connectors are ably used to mark transitions.	Very few errors. Sentence structure is varied, and vocabulary is advanced.
6	Insightful, clever analysis of the argument's flaws and fallacies.	Compelling, convincing examples and support develop a consistent, coherent critique. The analysis flows effortlessly and persuasively.	Very few errors. Sentence structure is varied, and vocabulary is precise, well chosen, and effective.

Try It Yourself

Use the following prompt to write your own timed essay.

Argument Topic

The following letter was sent to voters in a local school district.

"As you know, there is talk of consolidating our schools by closing Twin Lakes Elementary and moving those children to the larger school at Beaver Creek. This goes against what we know about the value of neighborhood schools. Studies show that small schools, defined as schools of 300 to 500 students, provide more in the way of teacher-student contact, which in turn improves student achievement. Twin Lakes, with just 95 students, offers our students even more. Studies also indicate that class size has a positive effect on student achievement at the primary grades. Twin Lakes averages only 16 students per grade level. Closing Twin Lakes may save a bit of money, but it will also mean certain failure for many of our students who are doing well right now."

Critique the reasoning used in this argument by examining assumptions, assessing evidence, and/or suggesting ways to make the argument stronger or easier to evaluate.

Turn off the grammar- and spell-checker on your word processor. Take 5 minutes to plan and outline your response. Leave 5 minutes at the end to check and revise your essay. Set your timer for 30 minutes.

When you finish, compare your essay to the following scored essays.

Argument Task Essay: Score of 6

This essay is fluent and coherent. It responds to the prompt insightfully and clearly by addressing the key flaws in the argument one by one and then suggesting some sensible ways the authors might improve that argument. There are no real errors in English usage or mechanics.

> Although it is clear that the authors of the letter
> are impassioned and sincere in their desire to save their
> tiny school, the evidence they use is seriously flawed.
> They offer two studies in support, both largely irrelevant
> to their thesis, and they conclude with a wild "slippery
> slope" suggestion that is not borne out by anything that
> has come before.
>
> Studies may indeed show that small schools, as
> suggested, provide more in the way of student-teacher
> contact, which in turn promotes academic achievement. Yet
> the authors point out the definition of small school: a
> school of from 300 to 500 students. That does not gibe
> with the population of Twin Lakes Elementary School, which
> houses only 95 students. Isn't it possible that a school
> can be too small--that the loss of economies of scale or
> teacher choice in such a tiny school might impact student
> achievement negatively? Using a study that features such
> different parameters from the situation at Twin Lakes is
> misleading at best.

The second study has to do with class size. Again, smaller is considered better, and Twin Lakes, with only 16 students per grade level, appears to be on target for small class size. However, not only does the letter not indicate the number that is optimal for class size, it does not provide any proof that class sizes are larger at the school at Beaver Creek.

Finally, the authors jump to the conclusion that because small schools and small classes improve student achievement, certain failure is imminent for students from Twin Lakes if they move to Beaver Creek. This is an enormous leap to take, not only because the use of the aforementioned two studies is questionable, but also because we are only told that small schools improve achievement, not that larger schools undermine it entirely.

The authors of the letter would be more credible if they found studies that proved that students performed best in schools as tiny as Twin Lakes, or that 16 students per grade is an optimal figure. Barring that, they might use anecdotal evidence to show how well Twin Lakes students perform compared to Beaver Creek students, as long as they could show that all other indicators (socioeconomic levels, education of parents, teacher training) were approximately equivalent. As it stands, the letter is impassioned but hardly convincing.

Argument Task Essay: Score of 4

This essay is competent and logical. It addresses the prompt by pointing out flaws in its assumptions, evidence, and conclusions and providing a couple of ideas for improving the argument. There are lapses in conventional English ("he or she use," "falacy"), but they do not interfere with a reader's understanding.

The letter wants people to think that closing Twin Lakes is a mistake. It uses certain assumptions, evidence, and conclusions, all of which contain some flaws.

The writer assumes that neighborhood schools have value. But he or she never shows exactly how that is so. We do not know what kind of neighborhood Twin Lakes is in, or how far students from Twin Lakes would have to travel out of their neighborhoods to reach Beaver Creek School. We do not know what he or she means by "value," whether it is home values or the value of having children close to home. The assumption is not supported by evidence.

The author does give some evidence that small schools are better. He or she use the study that shows that schools with 300–500 students have better student achievement. Yet Twin Lakes school has fewer students than that and doesn't fit the definition they give of small schools. Does the study (or the class size one) really fit the Twin Lakes situation at all? It is not clear that it does.

The author concludes that closing Twin Lakes would mean certain failure for the students who go there now, who are all doing fine right now. This is a falacy, because there is no evidence to suggest that those students are doing well just because of the school itself. They may be doing well because of their teachers, or because they are from educated families, or because of a host of other reasons. Some of those reasons may change when they move, but others will not. It is incorrect to conclude that such a move will mean instant failure for everyone. That sort of appeal to emotion is meant to rile up the reader, not to inform him or her in any meaningful way.

So the writer uses faulty assumptions, evidence, and conclusions to make a point. He or she would do better to talk about the impact on the community of closing a school, or about the "bit of money" saved by consolidation and how it doesn't make up for the loss of a community center.

Argument Task Essay: Score of 2

This essay is repetitive and disorganized. Instead of analyzing the existing argument, it merely repeats parts of it and fills in with the writer's own opinions and ideas. Many lapses in conventional English may interfere with a reader's understanding. Notice that this Score 2 essay is longer than the Score 4 essay that precedes it. Length does not matter; clarity and analysis do.

Twin Lakes is a small school that might be closed. The writer thinks that shouldn't happen.

A small school can be better for students because it is a better student-teacher ratio. That can be better for students by giving them more face-to-face time. Also small classes can offer students a lot of face-to-face time, leading to student acheivement.

Small schools are also better for academic acheivement from the authors point of view. A class of only 16 is better that classes that might be 25 or more at the bigger school that the little schools children might have to go to if the little school closes.

In my experience a small school that I went to as a young child was very good for my academic acheivement in that I was able to do a lot of extra circular things that allowed me to persue my passions about biology and other sciences. Because my teacher only had under 20 students, she was able to show me a lot more time and energy for my own needs. Like in Twin Lakes, I think we had just about that same number of students per class, which was very helpful for student acheivement. Later I went to a huge high school, it was hard to get any teacher attention with classes as big as 25 to 30 and maybe 300 students in the ninth grade. So if the school those Twin Lakes students go to is that big, it will definately be a problem.

One thing about the letter that might not be true is the end of the letter, where the writer says that closing the school might be "certain failure," which could be an exsageration. Maybe failure for some students who are used to the teachers attention, not for all the students. Some might even like to be in a bigger school with more extra circular activites or other students to be friends with. So it is wrong to think it would hurt every student, that's an exsageration.

In conclusion, small schools like Twin Lakes are probably better for student acheivement but not for everybody. If I lived in Twin Lakes I would vote against closing that small school which is probably a great thing for that small town to have.

ANALYTICAL WRITING DRILL 1

Use scratch paper to organize your response before you begin writing. Write your response on the pages provided, or type your response using a word processor with the spell- and grammar-check functions turned off.

Issue Topic

"Just as arranged marriages may stifle love, arranged careers may stifle productivity and creativity."

Discuss the extent to which you agree or disagree with the claim made above. Use relevant reasons and examples to support your point of view.

Argument Topic

"The trend toward buying local foods as a way of improving health, lowering energy costs by reducing trucking of foodstuffs, and keeping money in the local economy means that farmers' markets are the next big thing. Wayside Mall is going so far as to install an indoor farmers' market, featuring stalls from local farms. All indications are that the added traffic at Wayside Mall from people buying local produce will mean improved sales at most of the mall's stores, especially those on the first floor, where the farmers' market will be located."

Critique the reasoning used in this argument by examining assumptions, assessing evidence, and/or suggesting ways to make the argument stronger or easier to evaluate.

ANALYTICAL WRITING DRILL 2

Use scratch paper to organize your response before you begin writing. Write your response on the pages provided, or type your response using a word processor with the spell- and grammar-check functions turned off.

Issue Topic

"We called the twentieth century 'The American Century' for good reason, but the twenty-first century is something entirely different."

Discuss the extent to which you agree or disagree with the claim made above. Use relevant reasons and examples to support your point of view.

Argument Topic

The following letter to the editor appeared in a local newspaper.

"Our community has been ravaged by the rampant deer population, which is unchecked by predators or hunters. Deer carry the ticks that cause Lyme disease. They destroy vegetation in yards and along roads. Worst of all is the rise in deer-car accidents along most of our local roads. Accidents of that sort are up 25 percent over the past five years, with residents of the new Parkview Condominiums most grievously affected. Obviously, the deer population is out of control. Do we have to wait until someone is killed before we institute a sterilization plan? Sterilization is a humane way to curb the deer population. We will see the results as soon as next spring. I urge our mayor and common council to approve the sterilization plan at next month's meeting before it's too late."

Critique the reasoning used in this argument by examining assumptions, assessing evidence, and/or suggesting ways to make the argument stronger or easier to evaluate.

Answers and Explanations

Use the rubrics on pages 127 and 137 to analyze and score your writing. Better yet, give the rubric to a trusted friend or advisor and ask him or her to give you a thoughtful critique. Focus on the areas of your writing that need improvement.

PART IV

GRE ANALYTICAL WRITING AND VERBAL REASONING PRACTICE TESTS

PRACTICE TEST 1

2 Hours

ANALYTICAL WRITING 1. ANALYZE AN ISSUE

30 Minutes

1 Question

You will have 30 minutes to organize your thoughts and compose a response that represents your point of view on a given topic. Do not respond to any topic other than the one you select; a response to any other topic will receive a score of 0.

    Use scratch paper to organize your response before you begin writing. Write your response on the pages provided, or type your response using a word processor with the spell- and grammar-check functions turned off.

Issue Topic

> "The mark of an educated person is the ability to listen to and absorb an idea without necessarily accepting it as true."
>
> Discuss the extent to which you agree or disagree with the claim made above. Use relevant reasons and examples to support your point of view.

ANALYTICAL WRITING 2. ANALYZE AN ARGUMENT

30 Minutes

1 Question

You will have 30 minutes to organize your thoughts and compose a response that critiques the given argument. Do not respond to any topic other than the one given; a response to any other topic will receive a score of 0.

You are not being asked to discuss your point of view on the statement. You should identify and analyze the central elements of the argument, the underlying assumptions that are being made, and any supporting information that is given. Your critique can also discuss other information that would strengthen or weaken the argument or make it more logical.

Use scratch paper to organize your response before you begin writing. Write your response on the pages provided, or type your response using a word processor with the spell- and grammar-check functions turned off.

Argument Topic

A politician gave a speech in the 1990s that included this section.

"We cut taxes in this country eight years ago, yet federal revenues since that time have increased 20 percent. Not only that, but our unemployment rate is the lowest it has been in 15 years, and we are seeing a significant boom both in the housing industry and in the stock market. It should be clear to all thinking citizens that cutting taxes has a positive effect on the economy."

Critique the reasoning used in this argument by examining assumptions, assessing evidence, and/or suggesting ways to make the argument stronger or easier to evaluate.

▰▰ SECTION 1. VERBAL REASONING

30 Minutes

20 Questions

This section consists of three different types of questions: Sentence Equivalence, Text Completion, and Reading Comprehension. To answer the questions, select the best answer from the answer choices given. Circle the letter or word(s) of your choice.

Directions for Sentence Equivalence Questions: You are given a sentence with a blank replacing a missing word or words. For each sentence, select two answer choices that (1) complete the sentence in a way that makes sense and (2) produce sentences that are similar in meaning.

Example: Bone tumors once had a _____ prognosis because, unlike many other tumors, they tend to shed cancerous cells into the blood.

> A synthetic
>
> B survivable
>
> C surgical
>
> D dismal
>
> E widespread
>
> F bleak

Directions for Text Completion Questions: These questions consist of a short passage with one to three numbered blanks, indicating that something has been left out of the text. Complete the text by picking the best entry for each blank from the corresponding column of choices.

Example: The Norwegian elkhound is capable of hunting large game such as bear and elk. It corners its prey and uses its sharp bark to (i) _____ the beast (and alert the hunter to its position) while it uses its (ii) _____ to dodge and weave out of the way of hooves and claws.

Blank (i)	Blank (ii)
(A) distract	(D) vision
(B) attack	(E) size
(C) salute	(F) agility

Directions for Reading Comprehension Questions: The passages in this section are followed by several questions. The questions correspond to information that is stated or implied in the passage. Read the passage and choose the best answer for each question. You may be asked to choose one or more answers that fit. At other times, you will be asked to find the sentence in the passage that best answers the question.

For questions 1 to 4, select <u>two</u> answer choices that (1) complete the sentence in a way that makes sense and (2) produce sentences that are similar in meaning.

---

1. As the earth formed, enormous quantities of hydrogen and oxygen were trapped beneath the crust, and these elements _____ to form water.

   A aspired

   B evolved

   C required

   D combined

   E parlayed

   F united

2. Fredo's low test score seemed to Dr. Lewis to be an _____, and he comforted the boy, pointing out that he usually could be counted on to improve the class average.

   A anachronism

   B anomaly

   C apparition

   D ignominy

   E extremity

   F aberration

3. Carole has a particular aptitude for fine handiwork; on the other hand, she is surprisingly _____ at sports that require hand-eye coordination.

   A adept

   B repulsed

   C unskilled

   D incompetent

   E insignificant

   F helpful

4. In 1940, the largest earthquake to hit the state of New Hampshire measured 5.5 on the Richter scale and _____ minor damage to the surrounding area.

   A produced

   B concluded

   C distressed

   D caused

   E affected

   F evinced

Questions 5 and 6 are based on the following passage.

The gorilla has the misfortune to be native to an area that has been ravaged by war. Rwanda and the Congo are war-torn nations, and the resulting damage to habitat has affected gorillas as well as humans. Gorilla populations have also been ransacked by the Ebola virus, which has killed an estimated 90 percent of the gorilla population in each area of western and central Africa where it has been found.

The number one threat to gorillas, however, is human greed. Humans are burning down the forests where the last remaining gorilla families live. They are doing this to harvest charcoal, which is used to fuel cooking fires throughout the region. In addition, they are poaching the last remaining gorillas for meat and for their hands or other parts, which are considered a delicacy in Africa and are used medicinally in parts of Asia.

For each of questions 5 and 6, select one answer choice.

5. Which of the following best states the author's main point?

   (A) Gorillas are not designed for survival.

   (B) Poaching must be outlawed.

   (C) Humans put gorillas at risk.

   (D) We must protect our ape cousins.

   (E) Ebola affects everyone in Africa.

6. Based on information in the passage, about how many gorillas have survived Ebola in regions where the virus is prevalent?

   (A) about 1 percent

   (B) about 1 in 10

   (C) about half

   (D) nearly 9 in 10

   (E) nearly 4 in 5

Question 7 is based on the following passage.

Robert Scott's ill-fated Terra Nova expedition to the South Pole was a disaster on several fronts. First, his party was bested by that of Norwegian Roald Amundsen. Amundsen's group, making its second attempt, was well-equipped and prepared. They arrived at the pole more than a month before Scott's group did and returned safely to their base camp just a week after Scott's arrival at the pole. Second, on the way back, harsh weather and poor conditions killed every member of Scott's party. Third, although originally he was hailed as a hero, Scott's reputation was severely challenged more than half a century later when studies indicated that a combination of poor planning and hubris were responsible for Scott's failure.

Consider each of the choices separately and select all that apply.

7. According to the passage, Amundsen's and Scott's expeditions were similar in which of the following ways?

   A Both originated in Norway.

   B Both succeeded in reaching the pole.

   C Both suffered from poor planning.

For questions 8 to 10, complete the text by picking the best entry for each blank from the corresponding column of choices.

8. Inexpensive and (i) _____ available, aspirin has been used for decades to (ii) _____ fever and inflammation and to reduce pain.

Blank (i)	Blank (ii)
(A) readily	(D) minister to
(B) modestly	(E) enhance
(C) likewise	(F) transform

9. Although no one understands (i) _____ how some animals recognize that an earthquake is imminent, it is clear that they (ii) _____ stimuli that humans cannot detect.

Blank (i)	Blank (ii)
(A) adroitly	(D) create
(B) precisely	(E) sense
(C) manifestly	(F) realize

10. Contrary to popular belief, tulips are not (i) _____ to Holland. In fact, tulips did not arrive in Western Europe until the sixteenth century. While those first bulbs came from Turkey, where tulips have been cultivated since the early second century, the plants probably (ii) _____ in the rugged mountainous regions (iii) _____ the Black Sea.

Blank (i)	Blank (ii)	Blank (iii)
(A) indigenous	(D) matured	(G) beneath
(B) unique	(E) localized	(H) surrounding
(C) accustomed	(F) originated	(I) contained by

Questions 11 through 13 are based on the following passage.

Aluminum is the most abundant metallic element in the earth's crust, but it is never found naturally as an element. Instead, it always appears naturally in its oxidized form as a hydroxide we call bauxite. As with all mining of metals, bauxite mining presents certain hazards. Along with the usual mining issues of degraded soil and polluted runoff, chief among them is the omnipresent bauxite dust, which clogs machinery and lungs, sometimes for miles around the mining site. Jamaica and Brazil have seen widespread labor protests recently against the major bauxite mining companies. Nevertheless, the companies continue to insist that no link between bauxite dust and pervasive lung problems has been proved.

For each of questions 11 and 12, select one answer choice.

11. The passage suggests that the author would most likely believe that

(A) bauxite mining poses health problems

(B) the U. S. should use less aluminum

(C) Jamaican bauxite is the best quality

(D) most mining takes place near the equator

(E) aluminum is increasingly a bad investment

12. According to the passage, how is aluminum unusual?

    (A) Mining of it is a hazardous process.

    (B) It is not found in nature.

    (C) It has an oxidized form.

    (D) It is extremely rare.

    (E) It is infrequently metallic.

13. Underline the sentence that indicates that workers are starting to fight back against the dangers of mining.

> **For questions 14 through 16, complete the text by picking the best entry for each blank from the corresponding column of choices.**

14. The rediscovery of the *Titanic* was made during sea trials of a remote-controlled sled, the *Argo*, _____ descending to depths of 20,000 feet (6,100 meters).

(A)	having often
(B)	capable of
(C)	which could
(D)	in the process
(E)	after making

15. The sea snail known as Ida's miter lays eggs in capsules that_____ to rocky surfaces along the ocean floor.

(A)	coalesce
(B)	hatch
(C)	adhere
(D)	extricate
(E)	proceed

16. Unless you have recently _____ the Chesapeake Bay and viewed Sharps Island Light, you may not understand why the lighthouse is _____ to the Leaning Tower of Pisa. In 1977, an ice floe knocked the lighthouse _____, giving it its current cockeyed look.

Blank (i)	Blank (ii)	Blank (iii)
(A) resided in	(D) referred	(G) out of kilter
(B) appraised	(E) summoned	(H) overturnedensue
(C) cruised	(F) compared	(I) akimbo

Question 17 is based on the following passage.

The Udall family rivals the Kennedy family for longevity and widespread connections to U.S. politics. For over a century, Udalls have served in state and federal office, in the judiciary and in the Cabinet. David King Udall, a Mormon, had two wives. Four of his sons were politicians. John served as mayor of Phoenix in the 1930s. Don served on the Arizona state legislature. Jesse was chief justice of the Arizona Supreme Court following the death of his brother Levi, who also held that office. John's son Nick, like his father, was mayor of Phoenix. Jesse's son David was a city councilman in Mesa, Arizona. Jesse's sons Stewart and Mo served as U.S. congressmen from Arizona—Mo for 30 years! Stewart was named secretary of the interior under Kennedy and Johnson. His son Tom and two of Tom's cousins served in the U.S. Congress simultaneously.

Select one answer choice.

17. Why does the author most likely mention the Kennedy family in line 1?

(A) to draw a comparison between a well-known and a lesser-known political family

(B) to indicate that a serious rivalry existed between the Udalls and the Kennedys

(C) to show that political ambition and service are a strong American tradition

(D) to contrast Catholics and Mormons in terms of their public service

(E) to demonstrate the Udalls' importance to the legacy begun by the Kennedys

Question 18 is based on the following passage.

Avionics is a portmanteau word meaning "aviation electronics." It is a term that has evolved over the last 40 years as airplane instrumentation has evolved from mostly mechanical to largely electronic. Today, avionics makes up the large part of the cost of any aircraft. Guidance and navigation systems are integrated. Communications includes public address systems for communicating with passengers, intercoms for communicating with flight crews, and radio or SatCom for communicating with ground personnel. In addition, planes today have weather radar, lightning detectors, automatic flight control systems, and collision-avoidance systems. All of these systems must work in tandem in order for the plane to fly.

Select one answer choice.

18. Which of the following inferences about avionics is best supported by the passage?

(A) Within a decade, passenger planes will take off and land without human intervention.

(B) Soon passenger planes will include features that now appear only on military planes.

(C) Just 40 years ago, there were no electronic devices on passenger airplanes.

(D) As avionics becomes more common, the cost of manufacturing planes will decrease.

(E) A glitch in a plane's electrical system may be the greatest danger in flight today.

Questions 19 and 20 are based on the following passage.

Beaten down, the world against them, exhausted—such was the self-assessment of the Beat Generation, as defined by Jack Kerouac in a 1948 conversation that became part of a 1952 *New York Times* article. At that time, the Beats were in their infancy. In the early '40s, Kerouac attended Columbia University on a football scholarship, but a leg injury ended his football career and forced him to drop out of school. His brief sojourn with the merchant marine and the navy ended badly, and Kerouac limped back to New York to rejoin friends at Columbia, meeting student Allen Ginsberg and the older William S. Burroughs as he did so. Most of Kerouac's friends had come of age during World War II, just as Ernest Hemingway and his friends had done during World War I. Just as Hemingway's generation was "Lost," or estranged from their homeland, the new generation was "Beat." They found it impossible to find a place in the new, postwar economy. They lived in toxic, brutal poverty and moved constantly; many of them struggled to find publishers for their oddly constructed, turbulent writings.

Select one answer choice.

19. The author compares the Beat Generation to the Lost Generation in terms of their

    (A) poverty

    (B) openness

    (C) prolific output

    (D) alienation

    (E) antiwar stance

Consider each of the choices separately and select all that apply.

20. According to the passage, which of the following was true of the Beats?

    ☐A Most came of age during World War II.

    ☐B Many had a difficult time finding a publisher.

    ☐C They moved from place to place frequently.

STOP. This is the end of Section 1.

▀▀▀ **SECTION 2. VERBAL REASONING**

30 Minutes
20 Questions

This section consists of three different types of questions: Sentence Equivalence, Text Completion, and Reading Comprehension. To answer the questions, select the best answer from the answer choices given. Circle the letter or word(s) of your choice.

> <u>Directions for Sentence Equivalence Questions:</u> You are given a sentence with a blank replacing a missing word or words. For each sentence, select <u>two</u> answer choices that (1) complete the sentence in a way that makes sense and (2) produce sentences that are similar in meaning.

Example: Bone tumors once had a _____ prognosis because, unlike many other tumors, they tend to shed cancerous cells into the blood.

> A synthetic
>
> B survivable
>
> C surgical
>
> D dismal
>
> E widespread
>
> F bleak

> <u>Directions for Text Completion Questions:</u> These questions consist of a short passage with one to three numbered blanks, indicating that something has been left out of the text. Complete the text by picking the best entry for each blank from the corresponding column of choices.

Example: The Norwegian elkhound is capable of hunting large game such as bear and elk. It corners its prey and uses its sharp bark to (i) _____ the beast (and alert the hunter to its position) while it uses its (ii) _____ to dodge and weave out of the way of hooves and claws.

Blank (i)	Blank (ii)
Ⓐ distract	Ⓓ vision
Ⓑ attack	Ⓔ size
Ⓒ salute	Ⓕ agility

Directions for Reading Comprehension Questions: The passages in this section are followed by several questions. The questions correspond to information that is stated or implied in the passage. Read the passage and choose the best answer for each question. You may be asked to choose one or more answers that fit. At other times, you will be asked to find the sentence in the passage that best answers the question.

Questions 1 through 3 are based on the following passage.

Epitaph derives from the Greek words meaning "on the tombstone." An epitaph, therefore, is a short text honoring a deceased person. Although it may appear directly on a gravestone, often the word is used to describe a poem or speech given to celebrate the dead person's life. One famous epitaph, known as the Kohima epitaph for the battle that inspired it, goes as follows:

> When you go home, tell them of us, and say
> For your tomorrow, we gave our today.

It appears on a war memorial to commemorate British soldiers who fell in a 1944 battle in Japan. It echoes an ancient epitaph written to honor soldiers in the Spartan army:

> Tell them in Sparta, thou that passes by
> Here, faithful to her charge, her soldiers lie.

Some epitaphs are simply lists of key qualities of the deceased or principles he or she admired. Susan B. Anthony's, for example, reads "Liberty, Humanity, Justice, Equality." Others tell of the deceased person's contribution to the times. Scott Joplin's simple inscription says "American Composer." Some represent the person's own words, as in Edgar Allan Poe's "Quoth the Raven nevermore" or Frank Sinatra's "The Best Is Yet to Come." The most poignant are addressed to the deceased by a loved one, as this epitaph for Mark Twain's daughter Suzy:

> Warm summer sun, shine kindly here;
> Warm southern wind, blow softly here;
> Green sod above, lie light, lie light—
> Good-night, dear heart, good-night, good-night.

> **For each of questions 1 and 2, select one answer choice.**

1. The author mentions Susan B. Anthony to

   (A) show that American and English epitaphs are very much alike

   (B) indicate that not all epitaphs are coined for fallen soldiers

   (C) reflect on the life of a famous American heroine

   (D) provide one example of an epitaph that mentions principles

   (E) reveal some ways in which women's epitaphs resemble men's

2. The author's attitude toward the epitaph for Mark Twain's daughter may be described as

   (A) pained

   (B) tolerant

   (C) touched

   (D) amused

   (E) insensitive

> **Consider each of the choices separately and select all that apply.**

3. The author mentions which of the following varieties of epitaph?

   ☐ A quotations or statements made by the deceased

   ☐ B citations from famous operas, plays, or ancient literary works

   ☐ C descriptions of the deceased person's role or occupation

Question 4 is based on the following passage.

In slipcasting, liquid clay slip is poured into a plaster mold. The plaster absorbs much of the moisture, and then the cast is removed, fettled, and left to dry. The resulting unfired piece is known as greenware. The technique is best used for intricate shapes not easily formed by hand or on the potter's wheel.

> **Select one answer choice.**

4. Based on the passage, it can be inferred that fettling is a manner of

   (A) firing a pot

   (B) making a mold

   (C) trimming a cast

   (D) drying plaster

   (E) turning a wheel

> **For questions 5 through 7, complete the text by picking the best entry for each blank from the corresponding column of choices.**

5. Soap opera is so called due to its inception on the radio as a dramatic serial _____ by a soap manufacturer.

   (A) commenced
   (B) advocated
   (C) subsidized
   (D) retrieved
   (E) preceded

6. In ancient Chinese astronomy, the sun's path across the sky is divided into four parts, each assigned an animal symbol and _____ further into seven sections known as *mansions*.

   (A) construed
   (B) subjugated
   (C) specified
   (D) allotted
   (E) partitioned

7. Because of his (i) _____ career as a relief pitcher for the New York Yankees, people who follow the game (ii) _____ that Mariano Rivera will be inducted into the Baseball Hall of Fame (iii) _____ after he retires from baseball.

Blank (i)	Blank (ii)	Blank (iii)
(A) inconsistent	(D) await	(G) presently
(B) outrageous	(E) insist on	(H) shortly
(C) exceptional	(F) assume	(I) in advance

> ### Questions 8 and 9 are based on the following passage.

The bright star we call Sirius is really a binary star—a gigantic white star known as Sirius A and a far smaller dwarf called Sirius B. Sirius A is truly massive—about twice the size of our sun and around 25 times more luminous.

Seen with the naked eye, the two stars coalesce into a single bright object in the nighttime sky. Sirius's existence was recorded by the ancient Egyptians, who used its initial date of visibility—the date at which the earth's rotation moves it far enough from the glare of our sun to be clearly seen—as the basis for their calendar. Its extreme brightness frightened the ancient Greeks, who ascribed to it evil powers. It wasn't until 1844 that astronomer Friedrich Bessel determined that Sirius must have an invisible companion star, and in 1862, American Alvan Graham Clark finally observed the tiny Sirius B.

> ### Select one answer choice.

8. Which statement could most logically follow the final sentence in the passage?

   (A) The Romans liked to celebrate the setting of Sirius with a canine sacrifice.

   (B) We see Sirius as extraordinarily bright due to its proximity to Earth.

   (C) The name of the star comes from the ancient Greek word for "glowing."

   (D) More recently, orbital irregularities have suggested a third, even smaller companion.

   (E) Sirius is nicknamed the "Dog Star," as it is part of the Canis Major constellation.

> ### Consider each of the choices separately and select all that apply.

9. The passage suggests that Sirius A is unusual in which of the following qualities?

   A radiance

   B density

   C hue

Questions 10 through 12 are based on the following passage.

Judson Memorial Church, at the south end of Washington Square Park in Manhattan, is an example of the good that can happen when churches reach outward rather than remaining insular and limited. In the early part of the twentieth century, Judson housed a free medical and dental clinic, and its parish house became a welcoming home to foreign students following World War II. Not only does the church have a mission involving social outreach, but it also has a history of sponsoring the arts. The church offers art exhibitions, dance and theater performances, and rehearsal space. At one time or another, it has shown the works of then-unknown artists Claes Oldenburg, Jim Dine, Red Grooms, and Yoko Ono, among many others. The Judson Dance Theater, which rehearsed and performed there from 1962 through 1964, made the church the premier venue for postmodern dance in that era. Sam Shepard and Lanford Wilson premiered new plays in the meeting room of the church. Even today, those who do not attend the sermons on Sunday frequent the Judson for its showcasing of the arts.

Select one answer choice.

10. The author of the passage would most likely agree with which of these assertions about churches?

(A) "When I look for religion, I must look for something above me, and not something beneath." —Harriet Beecher Stowe

(B) "When one loses the deep intimate relationship with nature, then temples, mosques, and churches become important." —Krishnamurti

(C) "The church was not merely a thermometer that recorded ideas and principles of popular opinion, it was a thermostat that transformed the mores of society." —Martin Luther King, Jr.

(D) "All national institutions of churches, whether Jewish, Christian, or Turkish, appear to me no other than human inventions, set up to terrify and enslave mankind, and monopolize power and profit." —Thomas Paine

(E) "Do not let your deeds belie your words, lest when you speak in church someone may say to you, 'Why do you not practice what you preach?'" —St. Jerome

> **Consider each of the choices separately and select all that apply.**

11. What examples does the author include of Judson's "reaching outward"?

    - [A] the operation of a free clinic on church grounds

    - [B] its use as a haven for international students

    - [C] rehearsal space in the church for dancers and actors

12. Underline the sentence that indicates that Judson Memorial Church attracts visitors outside its own congregation.

> **For questions 13 through 15, complete the text by picking the best entry for each blank from the corresponding column of choices.**

13. Human Rights Watch, (i) _____ Helsinki Watch, and Amnesty International are two organizations that research and (ii) _____ human rights worldwide.

Blank (i)	Blank (ii)
(A) in lieu of	(D) advocate for
(B) erstwhile	(E) rail against
(C) formerly	(F) contravene

14. A lichen is not a single organism; it is a symbiotic (i) _____ made up at times of a fungus and an alga or, less (ii) _____, of a fungus and a cyanobacterium.

Blank (i)	Blank (ii)
(A) creature	(D) atypical
(B) composite	(E) documented
(C) divergence	(F) frequently

15. One of the most frequently performed operas today is Puccini's *La bohème*, (i) _____ loosely on a novel by Henri Murger. With an Italian libretto but a French (ii) _____ that refers to a region that is now part of the Czech Republic, the opera has received (iii) _____ since its initial performance with Arturo Toscanini conducting.

Blank (i)	Blank (ii)	Blank (iii)
(A) inspired	(D) score	(G) auspices
(B) rather	(E) title	(H) calumny
(C) based	(F) composer	(I) accolades

Question 16 is based on the following passage.

William Mark Felt, who for 30 years hid his whistle-blowing role as "Deep Throat" in the Watergate scandal, started working for the FBI in 1942 and rose rapidly through the ranks. His first important work was with the Espionage Section in World War II. Following the war, he was transferred to sites all over the country, wherever his expertise was needed, working on everything from background checks of nuclear plant workers to investigations of organized crime. Arriving back in Washington in 1962, he was promoted regularly, but when J. Edgar Hoover died suddenly, Felt was passed over for the directorship of the FBI, which instead went to a political appointee, Richard Nixon's friend L. Patrick Gray. When reporters Woodward and Bernstein began publishing facts about the Watergate burglary in the *Washington Post*, suspicion focused for a time on Felt, who had access to everything the FBI investigated. However, his constant denials and certain unanswered questions satisfied many that he had not been involved—right up until his self-revelation in 2005, apparently in hopes of a book deal.

Select one answer choice.

---

16. It can be inferred from the last sentence in the passage that

    (A) Felt's entire life before 2005 was based on a lie.

    (B) Felt's disclosure came as a shock to many people.

    (C) Felt revealed secrets out of a wounded pride.

    (D) Felt's revelation led to a lucrative contract.

    (E) Felt's confession of involvement was specious.

For questions 17 through 20, select <u>two</u> answer choices that (1) complete the sentence in a way that makes sense and (2) produce sentences that are similar in meaning.

---

17. In the year 1433, Venetian nobleman Pietro Loredan tried to become the doge of Venice, but he was defeated by the man who would be his chief _____ until the end of his life.

    [A] assistant

    [B] rival

    [C] correspondent

    [D] adversary

    [E] autocrat

    [F] conspirator

18. Founded in 1877 and located at the base of College Hill in Providence, the Rhode Island School of Design has a campus _____ that of Brown University.

   A reminiscent of

   B favored over

   C analogous to

   D bordering

   E enclosed within

   F contiguous to

19. The National Registry of Historic Places is our nation's _____ of buildings and sites considered worthy of preservation.

   A property

   B catalog

   C manifestation

   D verification

   E conferral

   F inventory

20. Yeats's poem "Sailing to Byzantium" clearly made a strong impression on a variety of readers—science fiction author Robert Silverberg _____ the title for his own award-winning novella, composer Peter Westergaard wrote a cantata based on the poem, and the Oscar-winning film *No Country for Old Men* draws its title from the poem's first line.

   A shaped

   B adopted

   C purloined

   D retained

   E lifted

   F fixed on

STOP. This is the end of Section 2.

GRE PRACTICE TEST 1 ANSWER KEY

Section 1

1. D, F

2. B, F

3. C, D

4. A, D

5. C

6. B

7. B

8. A, D

9. B, E

10. A, F, H

11. A

12. B

13. Jamaica and Brazil have seen widespread labor protests recently against the major bauxite mining companies.

14. B

15. C

16. C, F, G

17. A

18. E

19. D

20. A, B, C

Section 2

1. D

2. C

3. A, C

4. C

5. C

6. E

7. C, F, H

8. D

9. A

10. C

11. A, B, C

12. Even today, those who do not attend the sermons on Sunday frequent the Judson for its showcasing of the arts.

13. C, D

14. B, F

15. C, E, I

16. B

17. B, D

18. D, F

19. B, F

20. C, E

GRE PRACTICE TEST 1 ANSWERS AND EXPLANATIONS

Analytical Writing

Use the rubric in Chapter 10 to analyze and score your writing. Better yet, give the rubric to a trusted friend or advisor and ask him or her to give you a thoughtful critique. Focus on the areas of your writing that need improvement.

Section 1. Verbal Reasoning

1. **The best answer is D, F.** The elements did not *aspire* to something (choice A), which would indicate that they had conscious thought. Nor did they *evolve* (choice B) or *parlay* (choice E), which are actions we ascribe only to living things. Instead, they simply *combined* (choice D) or *united* (choice F) to create water.

2. **The best answer is B, F.** The clues are in the second half of the sentence. The student usually does well, he "can be counted on to improve the class average." Therefore, this grade is unusual; it is an *anomaly* (choice B) or *aberration* (choice F), a deviation from the norm. It is not an *anachronism* (choice A), or holdover from an earlier time. Nor does Dr. Lewis view it as an *ignominy* (choice D), or disgrace.

3. **The best answer is C, D.** The words *on the other hand* indicate that you are looking for a contrast to Carole's aptitude. The best contrasts are *unskilled* (choice C) and *incompetent* (choice D).

4. **The best answer is A, D.** What did the earthquake do? It *produced* (choice A), or *caused* (choice D), minor damage.

5. **The best answer is C.** The main point of the passage will be the point around which every paragraph in the passage is centered. The author never states that gorillas are not designed for survival (choice A). Choices B and D may be tacit conclusions one may draw from the passage, but they are not overtly suggested and are not the main point. Choice E may or may not be true, but it is not the main idea. Every part of the passage indicates that human behavior is harming the great apes in general and gorillas in particular, making choice C the best response.

6. **The best answer is B.** According to the second paragraph, in areas with Ebola, the virus wipes out 90 percent of the gorillas. That leaves 10 percent, or 1 in 10.

7. **The best answer is B.** Only Amundsen is Norwegian (choice A), and the author makes a point of calling his group "well-equipped and prepared," meaning that choice C would not apply to them. The only one that applies to both is choice B—both succeeded in reaching the South Pole.

8. **The best answer is A, D.** Aspirin is not only inexpensive, it is also *readily,* or easily, available (choice A). It does not *enhance,* or add to fever (choice E); nor does it *transform,* or change fever (choice F)—it *ministers to,* or treats, fever and inflammation, making choice D the right choice.

9. **The best answer is B, E.** No one exactly, or *precisely* (choice B), understands the mechanism by which animals detect, or *sense* (choice E), earthquake-related stimuli.

10. **The best answer is A, F, H.** First blank: The word *indigenous* (choice A) or *unique* (choice B) might work; the first means "native," and the second means "exclusive." However, noting the context of the rest of the passage indicates that it tells about where tulips come from, making *indigenous* a better response. Second blank: *Matured* (choice D) means "aged," which does not quite fit the context. *Localized* (choice E), or "were limited to," is really the opposite of what is meant here. The passage suggests that tulips *originated* (choice F), or "started off," in a place other than Holland. Third blank: The mountainous regions cannot be *beneath* (choice G) or *contained by* (choice I) the Black Sea, so they must be *surrounding* it (choice H).

11. **The best answer is A.** There is nothing to support choices B, C, or E, and choice D is not a question of belief. The author states, "As with all mining of metals, bauxite mining presents certain hazards," indicating that choice A is the best answer.

12. **The best answer is B.** Aluminum is abundant, but it is not found naturally and must instead be oxidized.

13. **The best answer is "Jamaica and Brazil have seen widespread labor protests recently against the major bauxite mining companies."** The fact that these are "labor" protests indicates that workers are fighting back.

14. **The best answer is B.** The Argo is *capable of* (choice B) descending quite far. None of the other choices works syntactically in the sentence.

15. **The best answer is C.** What do the capsules do? They *adhere,* or stick to, rocky surfaces.

16. **The best answer is C, F, G.** You might cruise the Chesapeake Bay to see the lighthouse, whereupon you would notice that it has been knocked *out of kilter* (choice G), meaning "awry." At that point, you might understand why the lighthouse is *compared* to (choice F) the Leaning Tower of Pisa; it would not be *referred* (choice D) to the Leaning Tower of Pisa, because that makes no sense syntactically.

17. **The best answer is A.** The author never suggests that there is a rivalry (choice B), nor is the point of the passage to contrast religious groups (choice D) or to show a continuum (choice E). Although choice C makes sense, it is not the purpose of the passage.

18. **The best answer is E.** Although the author mentions innovations, there is no hint that choice A is the next step. Military planes are not mentioned (choice B), and choice C is not accurate—there were electronic devices, just not as many. Since avionics makes up the large part of the cost of aircraft, it is doubtful that the cost will come down (choice D). The best answer is choice E—it is clear with all of these electronic systems guiding and assisting the plane that a glitch in electronics would be very dangerous.

19. **The best answer is D.** "Just as Hemingway's generation was 'lost,' or estranged," so were the Beats.

20. **The best answer is A, B, C.** All three details are mentioned directly, two of them (moving and difficulty finding publishers) in the final sentence.

Section 2. Verbal Reasoning

1. **The best answer is D.** The author includes examples of the epitaphs of certain Americans that fit certain parameters. Susan B. Anthony's lists four principles by which she led her life.

2. **The best answer is C.** Suzy Clemens's epitaph is described as one of the "most poignant," which implies that the author is touched by the words.

3. **The best answer is A, C.** Although many epitaphs do include citations from works of music or literature (choice B), they are not included as part of this passage.

4. **The best answer is C.** The cast is removed from a mold and fettled before it is left to dry. The only answer that fits the order of steps is choice C, "trimming a cast."

5. **The best answer is C.** The dramatic serial known as a "soap opera" was sponsored, or subsidized (choice C) by a soap manufacturer. This is the only choice that makes sense.

6. **The best answer is E.** The clue is *further*; once the sun's path is divided, it is then further partitioned.

7. **The best answer is C, F, H.** First blank: Rivera must have had an *exceptional* (choice C) career for people to expect his induction into the Hall of Fame. Second blank: People would not "await that" or "insist on that"—such constructions are ungrammatical. The answer must be choice F. Third blank: The sentence construction calls for *shortly* (choice H) rather than *presently* (choice G); "in advance after" (choice I) makes no sense at all.

8. **The best answer is D.** Consider the topic of the last sentence before deciding which sentence would most logically follow it. The last sentence discusses the discovery of the invisible companion, Sirius (choice B). The only sentence that follows logically is the one suggesting a third companion, choice D.

9. **The best answer is A.** The author never suggests that Sirius A is unusual in *density* (choice B) or *hue* (choice C), but the fact that it is "25 times more luminous" than our sun and possesses "extreme brightness" indicates that its *radiance* (choice A) is unusual.

10. **The best answer is C.** The entire passage is about "an example of the good that can happen when churches reach outward" into the community, making King's comment on the transformational power of churches and their connection to popular opinion the most relevant of the five choices.

11. **The best answer is A, B, C.** All of the examples given show that Judson Memorial Church reaches outward "rather than remaining insular and limited."

12. **The best answer is "Even today, those who do not attend the sermons on Sunday frequent the Judson for its showcasing of the arts."** The author means that the church attracts people outside its own congregation to its exhibits and performances.

13. **The best answer is C, D.** Human Rights Watch was *formerly* (choice C) called "Helsinki Watch." As their names suggest, the organizations *advocate for* (choice D) human rights rather than railing against such rights or contravening (disobeying) them.

14. **The best answer is B, F.** A lichen is not a *creature* (choice A) at all; it is a *composite* (choice B), or mixture, of two non-animal living things. Usually, these are a fungus and an alga; less *frequently* (choice F), they are a fungus and a bacterium.

15. **The best answer is C, E, I.** First blank: The opera is *based* (choice C) loosely on the novel; it could not be *inspired* loosely. Second blank: It is the *title* (choice E) that is French—*La bohème*, or Bohemia, is now part of the Czech Republic. Third blank: The fact that it is one of the most frequently performed operas indicates that it is popular and receives *accolades*, or rave reviews (choice I).

16. **The best answer is B.** Your answer must be based only on what can be inferred from the last sentence, which refers to Felt's final revelation in hopes of a book deal. Although he lied about his involvement for 30 years, this does not mean that his whole life was a lie (choice A); the passage shows that he did many legitimate things prior to Watergate. You might infer from material earlier in the passage that Felt revealed secrets due to his dismay at being passed over for advancement (choice C), but you cannot infer it from the final sentence. Although Felt may have hoped for a book contract, there is no indication here that he received a lucrative contract (choice D). The author does say that he revealed the information in hopes of a book contract, but it would be a great leap to infer that this means he was lying about his involvement (choice E). Since Felt's previous denials and some unanswered questions had convinced many people of his innocence, it's appropriate to assume that his disclosure surprised those same people, making choice B correct.

17. **The best answer is B, D.** Although several of the choices could work in context, only *rival* and *adversary* are synonyms.

18. **The best answer is D, F.** Again, where it is impossible to discern correct answers by looking at the context, find the ones that are synonyms. Only *bordering* and *contiguous to* mean the same thing.

19. **The best answer is B, F.** Both of the correct answers are nearly synonymous with *registry*.

20. **The best answer is C, E.** Silverberg might have *adopted* (choice B) or even *fixed on* (choice F) the title, but there are no synonyms for those words on the list of answer choices, syntactically, so neither B nor F is correct. The answer must be that he *purloined* (choice C) or *lifted* (choice E) the title, meaning that he stole it.

PRACTICE TEST 2

2 Hours

ANALYTICAL WRITING 1. ANALYZE AN ISSUE

30 Minutes
1 Question

You will have 30 minutes to organize your thoughts and compose a response that represents your point of view on a given topic. Do not respond to any topic other than the one you select; a response to any other topic will receive a score of 0.

Use scratch paper to organize your response before you begin writing. Write your response on the pages provided, or type your response using a word processor with the spell- and grammar-check functions turned off.

Issue Topic

> "When we assume that we already know the truth, we impede our own progress."
>
> Discuss the extent to which you agree or disagree with the claim made above. Use relevant reasons and examples to support your point of view.

ANALYTICAL WRITING 2. ANALYZE AN ARGUMENT

30 Minutes
1 Question

You will have 30 minutes to organize your thoughts and compose a response that critiques the given argument. Do not respond to any topic other than the one given; a response to any other topic will receive a score of 0.

You are not being asked to discuss your point of view on the statement. You should identify and analyze the central elements of the argument, the underlying assumptions that are being made, and any supporting information that is given. Your critique can also discuss other information that would strengthen or weaken the argument or make it more logical.

Use scratch paper to organize your response before you begin writing. Write your response on the pages provided, or type your response using a word processor with the spell- and grammar-check functions turned off.

Argument Topic

This is part of a lecture by a professor of political science.

"Forty years ago, the country of Byzantia started life as a parliamentary democracy, but shortly thereafter, it found itself at war with neighboring Yakistan. After spending the national coffers on arms, and sending most of its able-bodied youth to the front, Byzantia was plagued by shortages and inflation. To keep his people from rebelling while the war continued, Byzantia's president declared a state of emergency and installed himself as dictator, a position he still holds today. Now, the tiny nation of Molivia, established just five years ago as a parliamentary democracy, is threatened by its own neighbor, and is buying up arms and training soldiers rapidly. It is no stretch at all to imagine Molivia becoming a dictatorship within the decade."

Critique the reasoning used in this argument by examining assumptions, assessing evidence, and/or suggesting ways to make the argument stronger or easier to evaluate.

SECTION 1. VERBAL REASONING

30 Minutes
20 Questions

This section consists of three different types of questions: Sentence Equivalence, Text Completion, and Reading Comprehension. To answer the questions, select the best answer from the answer choices given. Circle the letter or word(s) of your choice.

Directions for Sentence Equivalence Questions: You are given a sentence with a blank replacing a missing word or words. For each sentence, select two answer choices that (1) complete the sentence in a way that makes sense and (2) produce sentences that are similar in meaning.

Example: Bone tumors once had a _____ prognosis because, unlike many other tumors, they tend to shed cancerous cells into the blood.

- A synthetic
- B survivable
- C surgical
- D dismal
- E widespread
- F bleak

Directions for Text Completion Questions: These questions consist of a short passage with one to three numbered blanks, indicating that something has been left out of the text. Complete the text by picking the best entry for each blank from the corresponding column of choices.

Example: The Norwegian elkhound is capable of hunting large game such as bear and elk. It corners its prey and uses its sharp bark to (i) _____ the beast (and alert the hunter to its position) while it uses its (ii) _____ to dodge and weave out of the way of hooves and claws.

Blank (i)	Blank (ii)
(A) distract	(D) vision
(B) attack	(E) size
(C) salute	(F) agility

<u>Directions for Reading Comprehension Questions:</u> The passages in this section are followed by several questions. The questions correspond to information that is stated or implied in the passage. Read the passage and choose the best answer for each question. You may be asked to choose one or more answers that fit. At other times, you will be asked to find the sentence in the passage that best answers the question.

For questions 1 through 4, select <u>two</u> answer choices that (1) complete the sentence in a way that makes sense and (2) produce sentences that are similar in meaning.

---

1. Marcus did not wish to _____ his friends into attending the lecture, but he feared that they would miss out on a marvelous opportunity if they failed to do so.

   A convince

   B collude

   C curtail

   D conjure

   E coerce

   F compel

2. After working overtime for weeks, Ms. Olivera hoped for a short _____ in which to spend time with her husband and children.

   A respite

   B breach

   C doldrums

   D hiatus

   E imbroglio

   F venture

3. Dolphins can hear sounds that are two octaves higher than any _____ by humans.

    A perceived

    B resonated

    C enabled

    D conducted

    E distinguished

    F expounded

4. G. K. Chesterton admired Charles Dickens's ability to be original even while describing the most _____ situations.

    A unique

    B demoralizing

    C hackneyed

    D capricious

    E banal

    F histrionic

Questions 5 and 6 are based on the following passage.

In linguistics, *metathesis* refers to the reversal of phonemes in a word. This can come about by accident, as in the common mispronunciation "aks" for *ask* or the common (and correct) pronunciation of *iron* as "i-orn." It may come about on purpose, as in various language games.

The Reverend Archibald Spooner, an Oxford dean, was known for his unintentional transpositions and gave his name to the particular metathesis he represented: *spoonerisms*. Most famous spoonerisms once attributed to Spooner are now believed to be apocryphal, but they are nevertheless amusing; for example, his supposed advice to a substandard student: "You have deliberately tasted two worms and will leave Oxford by the next town drain." Spoonerisms are funny when the metathesis involved changes one word into another, and they seem to lend themselves particularly well to off-color jokes.

Select one answer choice.

5. The author's claim that most spoonerisms are apocryphal could best be supported by the inclusion of

   (A) a list of transpositions attributed to the Reverend Spooner

   (B) examples of modern-day transpositions based on famous spoonerisms

   (C) interviews with his contemporaries denying their authenticity

   (D) Spooner's own letters to relatives, colleagues, and friends

   (E) metathesis statistics from linguists and speech teachers

Consider each of the choices separately and select all that apply.

6. Which of these might be an example of accidental metathesis?

   [A] Saying *interduce* instead of *introduce*

   [B] Saying *asterix* instead of *asterisk*

   [C] Saying *cause* instead of *because*

Question 7 is based on the following passage.

The United States has had a voluntary, professional armed forces for decades. However, even when we had conscription, the system was unbalanced and unfair, because the draft drew from only a subset of the citizenry. When George Washington intoned that "every citizen who enjoys the protection of a free Government . . . owes his personal service to the defense of it," he did not mean that only those males of a certain age who failed at other career paths should serve. Washington, with his classical education, no doubt agreed with Rousseau that the professional army led to the death of democracy in ancient Rome and was to be avoided in our new democracy if at all possible. There is no doubt that mandatory conscription is good for democracy—it levels the playing field and tells the world, "We're in this together, so bring it on!"

Select one answer choice.

7. Which of the following, if true, would most weaken the author's assertion about the value of mandatory conscription?

(A) a study showing that the military rank of mandatory draftees in the Swiss Army correlates to their education and poverty levels

(B) the discovery that volunteer troops often regret their decision, whereas conscripts take their service in stride

(C) the fact that most of the world's nations with volunteer armies are constitutional monarchies or republics

(D) the suggestion that current troop levels are so low that mandatory redeployments equate to de facto conscription

(E) the revelation that Washington's National Conscription Act exempted certain politicians and officials

> For questions 8 through 10, complete the text by picking the best entry for each blank from the corresponding column of choices.

8. Because twins are so (i) _____ physically, they will usually (ii) _____ similarly to the same diet.

Blank (i)	Blank (ii)
(A) analogous	(D) activate
(B) predictable	(E) respond
(C) advanced	(F) consume

9. Although we tend to (i) _____ the plague with medieval times, several cases a year still (ii) _____ in the American Southwest.

Blank (i)	Blank (ii)
(A) evoke	(D) traverse
(B) equate	(E) transpire
(C) associate	(F) transmogrify

10. The tradition of a bread or cake at a wedding is thousands of years old. The cake (i) _____ from a simple loaf of bread in Roman times, through sweet buns and meat pies in the nineteenth century, (ii) _____ to the wonders of today. While the tradition has been around for a long time, having a multi-tiered, white confection is (iii) _____ new.

Blank (i)	Blank (ii)	Blank (iii)
(A) distorted	(D) in anticipation	(G) comparatively
(B) seceded	(E) all the way	(H) assiduously
(C) evolved	(F) matched up	(I) ostensibly

Questions 11 through 13 are based on the following passage.

Thomas Bowdler, a self-appointed editor trained as a physician, created a children's edition of Shakespeare that omitted some characters completely, toned down language he considered objectionable, and euphemized such shocking situations as Ophelia's suicide—an accident in Bowdler's version. Today, of course, we know Bowdler not for his good works, but instead for the eponym derived from his good name. To *bowdlerize* is to censor or amend a written work, often with a connotation of prudishness. Bowdler was not alone. Even earlier, poet laureate Nahum Tate rewrote *King Lear*, banishing the Fool entirely and giving the play a happy ending. His version was staged regularly from the 1680s throughout the eighteenth century.

There is some indication that Bowdler's sister Harriet did the actual editing of Shakespeare's text. She was a poet and editor in her own right, and clearly more qualified than her brother to lay hands on the work of the bard of Avon. She may have published the expurgated edition anonymously before allowing her brother to take over the rights. If this is so, it is unsurprising that Harriet would not have wanted her name on the book. If the original Shakespeare were truly objectionable, then it would have been doubly so for a well-bred, unmarried Englishwoman of the day.

Select one answer choice.

11. The passage implies that Bowdler's sister was a more likely editor than he because

  (A) she would have been truly offended by Shakespeare's plots

  (B) Bowdler was known for his misuse of the English language

  (C) women of the time were more likely to read Shakespeare

  (D) unlike her brother, she was a published writer and editor

  (E) Bowdler himself was far too busy with his medical practice

12. Underline the sentence that indicates that the Bowdlers were not the first to alter Shakespeare's texts.

> **Consider each of the choices separately and select all that apply.**

13. Based on the information in this passage, all of these would be bowdlerization EXCEPT

    - A   translating a Japanese folktale into English

    - B   eliminating reference to witches from a fairy tale

    - C   burning copies of *The Satanic Verses*

> **For questions 14 through 16, complete the text by picking the best entry for each blank from the corresponding column of choices.**

14. It may seem that the only beneficiary in a predator-prey relationship is the predator, but in fact the prey benefits from having its population _____.

Ⓐ eradicated
Ⓑ regulated
Ⓒ underestimated
Ⓓ subsumed
Ⓔ safeguarded

15. In the past, the boarding school hired strict _____ and sticklers for rules and regulations; now its preference is for administrators with a background in social work.

Ⓐ partisans
Ⓑ sycophants
Ⓒ aspirants
Ⓓ martinets
Ⓔ denizens

16. The (i) _____ of today's communications devices would seem (ii) _____ to citizens of late-nineteenth-century America, for whom the occasional use of a candlestick telephone was more than sufficient. Then again, for the grandparents of those citizens, having a telephone in the home was an unimaginable (iii) _____.

Blank (i)	Blank (ii)	Blank (iii)
(A) ubiquity	(D) prosaic	(G) encroachment
(B) largesse	(E) noxious	(H) extravagance
(C) puissance	(F) outlandish	(I) digression

Question 17 is based on the following passage.

To banish sprawl and increase sustainability, many modern planners have turned to nodal development, in which new development is concentrated around centers of commerce and served by transit. The idea is to avoid the long-distance commute that consumes our downtime and infects our air with pollutants. However, as with every one-size-fits-all plan that is stuck in the moment, nodal development fails to appreciate certain realities of life in the twenty-first century. There are people who prefer to live isolated from others; if those people cultivate a garden and work at home, they can have less of a carbon footprint than a nodal dweller who flies on business twice monthly. Any planning must take into account how people want to live as well as how they should live, and it must incorporate a long-range view toward how that way of living might develop.

Consider each of the choices separately and select all that apply.

17. In the author's opinion, plans for nodal development are

    A   shortsighted

    B   irresponsible

    C   overly uniform

Question 18 is based on the following passage.

Today we know Gustav Mahler as a great composer, but in his own day he was valued more as a conductor of other men's works. As a conductor, he was a perfectionist, and his grueling rehearsals paid off in the stunning performances of the Vienna Court Opera. His renown as a conductor led later in life to posts in America with the New York Philharmonic and the Metropolitan Opera. In his off-hours, which were few, he worked on his own compositions, and his symphonies were performed from time to time, although to very mixed reviews. Following Mahler's death in 1911, his work fell into neglect, but a revival after 1950 and his influence on later musicians ensured his place in the pantheon of great European composers.

Select one answer choice.

18. Which of the following inferences about Mahler is best supported by the passage?

(A) Mahler's compositions are not as significant historically as was his ability to conduct.

(B) Although Mahler mainly conducted operas, his own compositions were all symphonic.

(C) Mahler always considered himself first and foremost a composer of symphonies.

(D) Despite an indifferent initial reception to Mahler's work, his oeuvre inspired others.

(E) Mahler's symphonies mirror his onstage perfectionism in their controlled dynamics.

Questions 19 and 20 are based on the following passage.

The use of inhaled anesthetics can be traced back as far as the medieval Moors, who used narcotic-soaked sponges placed over the nostrils of patients. Some 300 years later, in 1275, Majorcan alchemist Raymundus Lullus is supposed to have discovered the chemical compound later called ether. The compound, which would later have a brief but important run as the anesthetic of choice in Western medicine, was synthesized by German physician Valerius Cordus in 1540. Adding sulfuric acid, known at the time as "oil of vitriol," to ethyl alcohol resulted in the compound Cordus called "sweet vitriol."

During the next few centuries, ether was used by physicians for a variety of purposes. Its effectiveness as a hypnotic agent was well known, and a favorite pastime of medical students in the early nineteenth century was the "ether frolic," an early version of the drunken frat party. Nevertheless, no record of ether's being used as an anesthetic in surgery appears until the 1840s.

For each of questions 19 and 20, select one answer choice.

19. The statement in lines 5–7 that ether would "have a brief but important run as the anesthetic of choice in Western medicine" implies that the author believes that

   (A) ether was not a particularly good anesthetic

   (B) ether was not used long enough to judge its effectiveness

   (C) ether was effective during the period when it was used

   (D) ether was a noteworthy import from the East to the West

   (E) ether was used more by private citizens than by doctors

20. The author writes that Lullus "is supposed to have discovered" ether probably because

   (A) there is conflicting evidence about his discovery

   (B) Lullus did not really discover ether at all

   (C) although Lullus was meant to discover it, someone else actually did

   (D) no one can really "discover" a chemical compound

   (E) given Lullus's other achievements, he should have discovered it

STOP. This is the end of Section 1.

SECTION 2. VERBAL REASONING

30 Minutes
20 Questions

This section consists of three different types of questions: Sentence Equivalence, Text Completion, and Reading Comprehension. To answer the questions, select the best answer from the answer choices given. Circle the letter or word(s) of your choice.

Directions for Sentence Equivalence Questions: You are given a sentence with a blank replacing a missing word or words. For each sentence, select <u>two</u> answer choices that (1) complete the sentence in a way that makes sense and (2) produce sentences that are similar in meaning.

Example: Bone tumors once had a _____ prognosis because, unlike many other tumors, they tend to shed cancerous cells into the blood.

A synthetic

B survivable

C surgical

D dismal

E widespread

F bleak

Directions for Text Completion Questions: These questions consist of a short passage with one to three numbered blanks, indicating that something has been left out of the text. Complete the text by picking the best entry for each blank from the corresponding column of choices.

Example: The Norwegian elkhound is capable of hunting large game such as bear and elk. It corners its prey and uses its sharp bark to (i) _____ the beast (and alert the hunter to its position) while it uses its (ii) _____ to dodge and weave out of the way of hooves and claws.

Blank (i)	Blank (ii)
(A) distract	(D) vision
(B) attack	(E) size
(C) salute	(F) agility

Directions for Reading Comprehension Questions: The passages in this section are followed by several questions. The questions correspond to information that is stated or implied in the passage. Read the passage and choose the best answer for each question. You may be asked to choose one or more answers that fit. At other times, you will be asked to find the sentence in the passage that best answers the question.

Questions 1 to 3 are based on the following passage.

The origin of the American sports lovers' snack, the Buffalo chicken wing, is murky, but it almost certainly was first made in Buffalo, New York, and most probably at the Anchor Bar by co-owner Teressa BellisSimo. The wings are quick-fried, but it is the sauce, a combination of cayenne hot sauce and melted butter, that is especially memorable. Teressa served the wings with a cooling blue cheese dressing and celery side dish that is often imitated at Buffalo-style wings restaurants around the nation.

A lesser-known regional dish that also derives its name from its city of origin, Cincinnati chili is unique in its complete lack of the traditional chili powder or chili pepper. Its ingredients instead feature allspice, cocoa, and cinnamon, and the chili is served over spaghetti and topped with shredded cheese. It was developed by Macedonian immigrant brothers in their small Greek restaurant, and the Middle Eastern taste of this peculiar chili took off and brought the brothers local fame.

For each of questions 1 and 2, select one answer choice.

1. The primary purpose of the passage is to show that

   (A) Cincinnati chili is not universally recognized as a true chili

   (B) most sports lovers enjoy snacks that are spicy and unusual in origin

   (C) immigrant chefs are among America's most innovative and creative

   (D) obscure restaurateurs have made lasting contributions to American cuisine

   (E) cheese is an unexpected but satisfying ingredient in many snack foods

2. According to the passage, the author considers Buffalo wings to be

  (A) inspiring

  (B) unforgettable

  (C) derivative

  (D) irreproducible

  (E) prosaic

Consider each of the choices separately and select all that apply.

---

3. How are Cincinnati chili and Buffalo wings similar?

  [A] in their use of traditional spices

  [B] in their nationwide popularity

  [C] in their connection to local restaurants

Question 4 is based on the following passage.

As the name indicates, a heptathlon is an athletic competition featuring seven events. Unlike many such contests, the events included differ significantly for men and women. Both sexes compete (albeit independently) in high jump, long jump, and shot put, but at that point the competition diverges. Women run a 100-meter hurdle race in their first day of competition. Men run a 60-meter hurdle race in their second day. Women throw javelins; men polevault. Women run a 200-meter and 800-meter race; men run a 60-meter and 1000-meter race.

Select one answer choice.

---

4. Which statement could most logically follow the last sentence in this paragraph?

  (A) Jackie Joyner-Kersee is probably the United States's best-known heptathlete of either sex.

  (B) In addition, women compete outdoors; the men's heptathlon is traditionally held indoors.

  (C) The following track-and-field events appear in neither women's nor men's heptathlons: discus throw, relay race, and triple jump.

  (D) Athletes score points for each event in the competition, and at the end of two days, the one with the highest score is the winner.

  (E) Thirty years ago, the heptathlon took the place of the pentathlon as the main women's track-and-field combined event.

> **For questions 5 through 7, complete the text by picking the best entry for each blank from the corresponding column of choices.**

5. A cultivar is basically a variety of plant that has been selected for _____ characteristics such as disease resistance or ease of propagation.

   - (A) recessive
   - (B) eccentric
   - (C) advantageous
   - (D) putative
   - (E) ineffectual

6. Although we know Samuel Coleridge for his poetry, at the time of his writing, his criticism was probably even _____.

   - (A) less celebrated
   - (B) better summarized
   - (C) higher quality
   - (D) more consequential
   - (E) greater magnitude

7. Crowd theory looks at the (i) _____ of people acting collectively. For example, Freud's nephew promoted the use of the psychology of the unconscious to (ii) _____ public opinion. Contagion theory suggests that being in a crowd causes people to act a certain way, (iii) _____ convergence theory states that people who want to act a certain way tend to form crowds.

Blank (i)	Blank (ii)	Blank (iii)
(A) behavior	(D) employ	(G) whereas
(B) capacity	(E) vanquish	(H) moreover
(C) quandary	(F) manipulate	(I) nonetheless

Questions 8 and 9 are based on the following passage.

The peculiar balls of light that World War II fighter pilots termed *foo fighters* were almost certainly ball lightning or a form of St. Elmo's fire, and not the UFOs some have posited. The fact that the light seemed to follow the aircraft makes St. Elmo's fire more likely than the lightning. A sort of electrical discharge from planes' wingtips has been documented, and this would explain the fact that the lights appeared, stayed with the planes, and then vanished without warning. Pilots could not outmaneuver them; the lights stayed even with their planes and managed to mimic the planes' speed and altitude. This could be explained if the lights were caused by harmless ionization of the air around the plane. Because electrical fields are more concentrated along curved surfaces, and the tighter the curve, the higher the concentration, it makes sense that such lights would appear at the wingtips of planes.

Select one answer choice.

8. Which of the following findings best supports the author's hypothesis?

   (A) One so-called foo fighter appeared to move thousands of miles per hour, far outstripping the plane it passed over.

   (B) An airplane over the South Pacific encountered glowing objects that caused its engines to fail temporarily.

   (C) An Australian pilot reported a large fiery object that stayed with his plane momentarily before turning away and diving into the sea.

   (D) The gunner of a B-29 managed to shoot down and disintegrate one of the mysterious balls of fire.

   (E) Pilots thought the foo fighters were secret German aircraft until Japanese and German pilots reported similar sightings.

Consider each of the choices separately and select all that apply.

9. Based on the last sentence of the passage, you might expect St. Elmo's fire to appear along

   A the distant horizon

   B the top of a ship's mast

   C the steeple of a church

Questions 10 to 12 are based on the following passage.

The opposite of free verse is, of course, fixed verse, in which the form of the poem is set ahead of time. Instead of, as Frost once described free verse, "playing tennis without a net," poets are required to adhere to rules involving meter, rhyme scheme, and length. From the Japanese haiku to the Arabic ghazal, from the Greek ode to the Chinese sanqu, fixed verse is both ancient and modern, both traditional and innovative. Although it is obviously possible to be creative within the structure of fixed verse, as Shakespeare was with the sonnet or Pound with the sestina, the rigidity of form may stifle originality in students who are just dipping their toes into the world of poetry. Therefore, some creative writing teachers sensibly prefer to start students off with just a theme and a brainstormed list of describing words rather than, for example, having them try their hands at a daunting villanelle.

Select one answer choice.

10. The references to Shakespeare and Pound are intended by the author to

   (A) provide imaginative alternatives to traditional free verse

   (B) specify exemplars of inventiveness despite the constraints of form

   (C) suggest that inspiration may be found in disparate venues

   (D) remind the reader that poetry's form may follow its function

   (E) contrast the talent of celebrated poets with the incapability of students

Consider each of the choices separately and select all that apply.

11. According to the passage, the author considers the villanelle to be

   [A] a difficult form of fixed verse

   [B] more complex than the ghazal

   [C] inappropriate for beginners

12. Underline the sentence that clarifies the elements of fixed verse.

> **For questions 13 through 15, complete the text by picking the best entry for each blank from the corresponding column of choices.**

13. The term *astral projection* is used to refer to an out-of-body experience in which the consciousness leaves the (i) _____ body to travel in the astral plane, a plane of existence (ii) _____ by classical, medieval, Eastern, and mystic philosophies and religions.

Blank (i)	Blank (ii)
(A) corporeal	(D) prefigured
(B) detached	(E) deemed
(C) presumptive	(F) postulated

14. The larvae of some hoverflies are saprotrophs, eating detritus, or the (i) _____ plant or animal matter they find in soil or stream; others are insectivores that (ii) _____ thrips and aphids.

Blank (i)	Blank (ii)
(A) nugatory	(D) evade
(B) decaying	(E) prey on
(C) dynamic	(F) subsume

15. The scuppernong, an unusually large bronze-colored grape that is (i) _____ in the American southeast, was named for the river in North Carolina where it was first described by explorer de Verrazzano in 1524. Like all muscadines, it is quite (ii) _____ of pests, making it a hardy fruit, at least in (iii) _____ climes like that of North Carolina.

Blank (i)	Blank (ii)	Blank (iii)
(A) singular	(D) emancipated	(G) perpetual
(B) potent	(E) debilitated	(H) temperate
(C) rife	(F) tolerant	(I) cultivated

Question 16 is based on the following passage.

The patently random movement of particles in water is known as Brownian motion, so named because of the botanist who first wrote about it. Scottish scientist Robert Brown was examining pollen grains under a microscope when he noted tiny particles in their vacuoles exhibiting a haphazard, jerky motion. Briefly, until he later observed a similar motion in particles of dust, he posited that something in the pollen was alive. Later observers determined that the irregular, back-and-forth, up-and-down motion occurs when particles of less than one-tenth of a micron in size are bombarded by the entirely random movement of atoms and molecules in the air or water. Under a microscope, the particles are visible, but the atoms and molecules batting them about are not. In one of his early papers, Albert Einstein observed particle motion and was able to extrapolate from that the size of the molecules affecting the particles.

Select one answer choice.

16. The activity described in the passage most closely resembles

  Ⓐ multiple Frisbee players tossing a disc back and forth

  Ⓑ popcorn popping inside a bag in a microwave oven

  Ⓒ tiny wrasse fish cleaning the gills of a larger fish

  Ⓓ football fans batting a huge beach ball around a stadium

  Ⓔ a vacuum cleaner sucking up dust balls from under a bed

For questions 17 through 20, select <u>two</u> answer choices that (1) complete the sentence in a way that makes sense and (2) produce sentences that are similar in meaning.

17. In various European countries and members of the United Kingdom as well as in the United States, April Fools' Day is a time for _____ pranks carried out by otherwise rational individuals.

  A convoluted

  B puerile

  C disingenuous

  D sophomoric

  E despotic

  F conniving

18. Despite the formality of their office, presidents James Carter and William Clinton went by the _____ Jimmy and Bill, respectively.

   A ripostes

   B façades

   C sobriquets

   D phalanges

   E anecdotes

   F monikers

19. Steam locomotives _____ rail transportation for at least 150 years, from the dawn of the nineteenth century through the middle of the twentieth.

   A dominated

   B represented

   C reclaimed

   D touted

   E ruled

   F supplied

20. Recently, gas drilling has become a _____ issue in upstate New York, with residents taking sides on whether or not to lease land and allow hydrofracking to go forward.

   A prominent

   B diffident

   C contentious

   D divisive

   E laudable

   F putative

STOP. This is the end of Section 2.

GRE VERBAL PRACTICE TEST 2 ANSWER KEY

Section 1

1. E, F

2. A, D

3. A, E

4. C, E

5. C

6. A, B

7. A

8. A, E

9. C, E

10. C, E, G

11. D

12. Even earlier, poet laureate Nahum Tate rewrote *King Lear*, banishing the Fool entirely and giving the play a happy ending.

13. A, C

14. B

15. D

16. A, F, H

17. A, C

18. D

19. C

20. A

Section 2

1. D

2. B

3. C

4. B

5. C

6. D

7. A, F, G

8. E

9. B, C

10. B

11. A, C

12. Instead of, as Frost once described free verse, "playing tennis without a net," poets are required to adhere to rules involving meter, rhyme scheme, and length.

13. A, F

14. B, E

15. C, F, H

16. D

17. B, D

18. C, F

19. A, E

20. C, D

GRE PRACTICE TEST 2 ANSWERS AND EXPLANATIONS

Analytical Writing

Use the rubric in Chapter 10 to analyze and score your writing. Better yet, give the rubric to a trusted friend or advisor and ask him or her to give you a thoughtful critique. Focus on the areas of your writing that need improvement.

Section 1. Verbal Reasoning

1. **The best answer is E, F.** You might turn the sentence around to examine its meaning more closely. Because Marcus feared his friends would miss out on an opportunity if they did not attend the lecture, he might [missing word] his friends to attend, even though it was something he didn't wish to do. He would not shrink at "convincing" them (choice A). *Collude* (choice B) means "to scheme with," so it does not fit the context. *Curtail* (choice C) means "to restrain," and *conjure* (choice D) means "to summon up (as in a magic trick)." Neither works in this sentence. Only *coerce* and *compel*, meaning "to force or put pressure on," fit with Marcus's hesitation.

2. **The best answer is A, D.** Ms. Olivera is tired of working so hard, so she hopes for a *respite*, a *hiatus*, or a break. She would not be likely to hope for a *breach* (separation), *doldrums* (period of boring inactivity), an *imbroglio* (embarrassing situation), or a *venture* (business undertaking).

3. **The best answer is A, E.** Dolphins and humans are being compared in regard to their hearing. Humans are not *resonating* (choice B), *enabling* (choice C), *conducting* (choice D), or *expounding* (choice F) the sounds; they are *perceiving* them (choice A) or *distinguishing* (choice E) them—or, rather, failing to perceive or distinguish them.

4. **The best answer is C, E.** Although Dickens often described situations that were demoralizing (B), the synonyms that fit the context are *hackneyed* (choice C) and *banal* (choice E)—Dickens could be original even when describing such everyday events.

5. **The best answer is C.** If most spoonerisms are apocryphal, or fictional, that would not be proved by a list of attributed transpositions (choice A), which would simply seem to support their authenticity. Examples of modern-day transpositions (choice B) would do nothing to support or deny the authenticity of spoonerisms, and Spooner's letters (choice D) would not help, because his transpositions, if they existed, were oral, not written. Statistics (choice E) would not tell anything about Spooner himself. Interviews with people who knew Spooner (choice C) would be the best way to settle the issue one way or the other.

6. **The best answer is A, B.** Saying *cause* instead of *because* (choice C) is an example of *aphaeresis*, the loss of the initial part of a word. The other two examples show accidental transpositions of phonemes.

7. **The best answer is A.** The author's assertion is that mandatory conscription is good because it levels the playing field. If a system of mandatory conscription is shown instead to have facilitated inequities, that would weaken the assertion. The other statements do not directly belie the author's point of view.

8. **The best answer is A, E.** Twins are remarkably similar, or *analogous* (choice A) physically. This similarity causes them to *respond* (choice E) similarly to the same diet.

9. **The best answer is C, E.** We would not *equate* the plague with medieval times (choice B); that implies that the two are equal. We might *associate* the two (choice C). Cases may still occur, or *transpire* (choice E) in the American Southwest. They do not *traverse* (go across) or *transmogrify* (alter in form).

10. **The best answer is C, E, G.** First blank: The only word that fits the context of the sentence is *evolved*, meaning "developed." Second blank: "from a simple loaf of break through sweet buns and meat pies *all the way* to the wonders of today" is the only wording that makes sense here. Third blank: The white, multitiered confection is not *assiduously* (tirelessly) new, nor is it *ostensibly* (supposedly) new. It is *comparatively* (relatively) new.

11. **The best answer is D.** Bowdler himself was trained as a doctor; the passage makes clear that he was not an editor. His sister, however, was a poet and editor, and therefore was more likely than he to have made the editorial changes that led to the revised Shakespearean texts. There is no evidence in the passage to support choice B, C, or E, and although there is some implication that choice A is true, it does not explain why she would have been a more likely editor than he.

12. **The best answer is "Even earlier, poet laureate Nahum Tate rewrote *King Lear*, banishing the Fool entirely and giving the play a happy ending."** This sentence proves that the Bowdlers were not the first to alter Shakespeare's texts—Tate did it "earlier."

13. **The best answer is A, C.** Remember that the answer will *not* be an example of bowdlerization. First, you must find the definition of bowdlerization in the text: "to censor or amend a written work, often with a connotation of prudishness." Choice A is not an example of this; simply translating from one language to another requires neither censorship nor amendment. Choice C is not an example either; although some may say that book burning is a radical form of censorship, it does not fit the definition here. Only choice B, which deals with the censorship of a detail in a text, fits the definition.

14. **The best answer is B.** Prey could not benefit from being *eradicated* (choice A) or win by being *underestimated* (choice C). *Subsumed* (choice D), meaning "included within a larger group," does not fit the context here. If prey is *safeguarded*, or protected (choice E), that's not part of a predator-prey relationship. Only choice B fits both parts of the sentence.

15. **The best answer is D.** Look at both parts of the sentence to choose the best response. The school now looks for social workers, but in the past, it hired strict disciplinarians, or *martinets* (choice D).

16. **The best answer is A, F, H.** Today's communications devices are *ubiquitous*, meaning "found everywhere." This would have seemed strange, or *outlandish* (choice F), to long-ago citizens. Those citizens used telephones occasionally, but for their grandparents, that would have been a shocking *extravagance* (choice H).

17. **The best answer is A, C.** The author suggests that plans for nodal development do not incorporate a long-range view, making them shortsighted (choice A). In addition, the plan strikes the author as "one-size-fits-all," or overly uniform (choice C). Despite the author's qualms, nowhere does she describe the plan as irresponsible (choice B), which would imply a level of recklessness that she does not attribute to modern planners.

18. **The best answer is D.** The passage notes that we now know Mahler as a great composer, making choice A incorrect. There is no indication that Mahler's compositions were all symphonic (choice B), although the passage does mention performances of his symphonies. Because Mahler is portrayed as a perfectionist conductor, choice C seems doubtful, and there is no support at all for choice E. The author does suggest that Mahler, despite his mixed reviews, influenced later musicians, making choice D the best answer.

19. **The best answer is C.** Ether's run is described as "brief but important," implying that despite its short reign as the anesthetic of choice, it was an effective choice. There is no support in the passage for any of the other answer choices.

20. **The best answer is A.** "Supposed to have discovered" means that Lullus is "said to have discovered." It implies that there is not a lot of corroborating evidence; if there were, the author would have simply said "discovered." Choice B may be true, but for the time being, the author is implying that Lullus may or may not have made the discovery.

Section 2. Verbal Reasoning

1. **The best answer is D.** The author never suggests that Teressa Bellissimo was an "immigrant chef" (choice C); in fact, she was born in the United States. A better response is choice D, because both regional dishes mentioned emerged from the kitchens of little-known chefs.

2. **The best answer is B.** The author says that the dish is memorable. Choice B is the best restatement of this.

3. **The best answer is C.** Both dishes came from local restaurants and grew in popularity, but only the Buffalo chicken wing can be considered a nationwide treat.

4. **The best answer is B.** To answer this, look at the passage as a whole. Its purpose is to show the way the men's and women's heptathlons differ. Only choice B maintains this purpose.

5. **The best answer is C.** Disease resistance and ease of propagation would be *advantageous* (C), not *recessive* (not dominant), *eccentric* (unconventional), *putative* (alleged), or *ineffectual* (unimpressive).

6. **The best answer is D.** Test each of the answers in the sentence. The only one that makes sense both semantically and syntactically is choice D.

7. **The best answer is A, F, G.** First blank: Reading the next two sentences indicates that crowd theory looks at *behavior* (choice A). Second blank: What might you wish to do to public opinion? You would not want to *vanquish*, or defeat it (choice E), and employing, or using, it (choice D) would not be very meaningful. It might be useful to *manipulate*, or influence it, however, making choice F the best answer. Third blank: The sentence construction calls for a contrast between contagion and convergence theories, making *whereas* (choice G) the best choice.

8. **The best answer is E.** Since the author's hypothesis is that the balls of light were a form of St. Elmo's fire, anything that suggests that the light moved faster than the planes (choice A), caused mechanical problems (choice B), took an unexpected turn (choice C), or could be demolished (choice D) would contradict this. Only choice E is neutral; it does not prove the theory, but it does not disprove it, either.

9. **The best answer is B, C.** St. Elmo's fire concentrates along curves and tips of objects, meaning that masts (choice B) and steeples (choice C) are likely sites.

10. **The best answer is B.** The author uses Shakespeare and Pound to show that "it is obviously possible to be creative within the structure of fixed verse."

11. **The best answer is A, C.** The author calls the villanelle "daunting," which indicates that choice A is correct, and she suggests that teachers are more sensible to start their students elsewhere, making choice C correct as well. However, she never hints that a ghazal is less challenging (choice B).

12. **The best answer is "Instead of, as Frost once described free verse, 'playing tennis without a net,' poets are required to adhere to rules involving meter, rhyme scheme, and length."** Meter, rhyme scheme, and length are three elements of fixed verse.

13. **The best answer is A, F.** The consciousness leaves the *corporeal*, or physical, body (choice A) to travel on a plane that was *postulated*, or hypothesized (choice F), by many cultures.

14. **The best answer is B, E.** Detritis is *decaying* (choice B) matter, not *nugatory* (trivial) or *dynamic* (lively) matter. You would expect insectivores to *prey on* (choice E), or eat, thrips and aphids, which are insects.

15. **The best answer is C, F, H.** First blank: The grape is *rife* (choice C), or common, in the Southeast. Second blank: If it is hardy, it must be *tolerant* (choice F) of pests. Third blank: A clime, or climate, would not be *perpetual* (choice G) or *cultivated* (choice I), but it might be *temperate*, or mild (choice H).

16. **The best answer is D.** Think about the motion that is described: Small particles work randomly to bombard a larger, round object, tossing it this way and that in a haphazard way. Only choice D fulfills each aspect of this description.

17. **The best answer is B, D.** Again, where it is impossible to discern correct answers by looking at the context, find the ones that are synonyms. Only *puerile* and *sophomoric* mean the same thing—"immature."

18. **The best answer is C, F.** To get this one right, you must know the vocabulary. *Sobriquets* (choice C) and *monikers* (choice F) are nicknames. *Ripostes* (choice A) are wisecracks, *façades* (choice B) are veneers, *phalanges* (choice D) are fingers, and *anecdotes* (choice E) are stories.

19. **The best answer is A, E.** Steam locomotives may have *represented* (choice B) rail transportation, but the only answers that are synonymous are *dominated* (choice A) and *ruled* (choice E).

20. **The best answer is C, D.** It may be a *prominent* (choice A) or even a *laudable* (choice E) issue, but the only synonyms here are *contentious* (choice C) and *divisive* (choice D), both of which echo the fact that residents are "taking sides."